Design Project Management

Griff Boyle

ASHGATE

Published by
Ashgate Publishing Limited
Wey Court East
Union Road
Farnham
Surrey GU9 7PT
England

Ashgate Publishing Company
Suite 420
101 Cherry Street
Burlington, VT 05401–4405
USA

Ashgate website: http://www.ashgate.com

British Library Cataloguing in Publication Data
Boyle, Griff
   Design project management
   1. Design, Industrial - Management 2. Project management
   I. Title
   658.4'04

Library of Congress Cataloging-in-Publication Data
Boyle, Griff.
    Design project management / Griff Boyle.
       p. cm.
    Includes bibliographical references and index.
    ISBN 0-7546-1831-5
       1. Design, Industrial. 2. Project management. I. Title.

TS171 .B69 2002
658.5'752--dc21

2002025860

ISBN 0 7546 1831 5
ISBN 978 0 7546 1831 7

Reprinted 2009

Mixed Sources
Product group from well-managed
forests and other controlled sources
www.fsc.org Cert no. SA-COC-1565
© 1996 Forest Stewardship Council
FSC

Printed and bound in Great Britain by
MPG Books Ltd, Bodmin, Cornwall.

Contents

List of figures and tables

FIGURES

TABLES

1 The key to design management

INTRODUCTION

This book about design project management has been written primarily for client organisations who may work with designers regularly, or who may have been asked to work with designers for a one-off project while carrying out their own 'core' non-design business duties. It has not been written primarily for designers, although designers may also find it helpful. It sets out to explain and demystify the design process for the non-designer, making analogies wherever possible with more familiar everyday business experiences and processes, illustrating a step-by-step methodology for integrating design into a business. It is a client's guide to initiating, setting up, directing and managing successful design projects. Examples are drawn mainly from multidisciplinary projects for the built environment, but the approach and principles described are applicable to other design projects.

Underlying the book is the desire to promote clarity, communication and integration of effort between all parties engaged on a design project. At its heart is the belief that these factors will make possible a match between the end result expected from the project and the end result achieved. Thus all contributors must share the same set of aspirations and expectations simultaneously. While recognition of the need for clarity has motivated this book, the core significance of shared design project values optimises the creative and business potential of the project.

If a designer is asked to identify the most important factors contributing to a successful design project, the following will probably appear repeatedly among the top four answers suggested:

- A good budget
- A good brief
- A good client
- An appropriate timescale.

While there may be some disagreement regarding the exact order of priority, there is likely to be little debate about the ability of each factor to influence a design project either for good or ill. However, the factors noted above fall into two distinct categories. On the one hand, there are 'hard factors' – finance and programme. These are usually easily objectified and determined through a business imperative. On the other hand there are 'soft factors' – a 'good' client and a 'good' brief. These are far less easy to establish or agree in objective terms, and whose perspective should be used?

Beginning a book professing to be a client's guide to successful design project management therefore demands that we start with establishing some fundamental definitions regarding design, design projects, success, good clients, good design briefs and so on.

- What do we mean by design?
- What do we mean by design project management?
- Who judges what we mean by success? Can the success be measured?
- What makes a good client? Brief? Budget? Programme?

Each of these questions is considered as the book sets out a first-principles sequential map of the areas of concern that are always present in any design project. It aims to provide clients from any area of business with the tools necessary to understand designers and the design process. It provides checklists for each major stage in the evolution of a design project, and brief case studies to illustrate points of principle. The book seeks simultaneously to recognise the unique nature of individual design projects and strongly emphasise the common patterns underlying each.

If after reading this book only one piece of information is to be retained by the reader it should be this:

The key to successful design rests with the client, not with designers.

WHAT DO WE MEAN BY DESIGN?

For the purposes of this book successful design is not viewed from the perspective of creating purely personal statements, such as those that arise, say, from the completion of domestic-scale interior design projects. Here the outcome of the design may be viewed by one party to be a success with no visible, objective criteria to enable others to form an assessment; that is, there is often no right or wrong view, other than a response based on personal taste. This book views design from a broader perspective, considering how it may best be integrated into the wider spectrum of meeting the business needs of an organisation, where success may be assessed and indeed measured through strict business criteria. It is important to establish such key factors for a book such as this, as it should be possible to measure the success of the book by judging its usefulness to the reader against the criteria established.

Design, defined in its broadest sense, is an activity we all undertake many times every day. In getting on with daily life, we all design and redesign processes and activities to fulfil our own needs, from children crossing roads to business people evaluating complex strategic business processes. Design is an activity that goes well beyond a concern with form and surface and the purely visual criteria with which it is often most readily associated by the public, and too often by designers themselves. Design is the activity of turning a 'need' into a solution, a 'concept' into a reality. The solution may have or may not have a physical form, but it will certainly have a purpose, and the emphasis in this book is on design purpose, and more specifically the holistic 'fitness for purpose' achievable through integrating design properly into a host business.

A visually led approach to evaluating design often attempts to position it as an activity to which the untrained are unlikely to be in a position to contribute, or perhaps even understand – an activity closely aligned to having 'talent at art' or 'good taste'. This is a position sometimes unfortunately reinforced by designers themselves through the production of drawings and the use of language which does not adequately communicate to the layman – a position often driven by criteria amounting to little more than self-satisfaction, and the wish to express values considered important by peers.

The position of design as 'elitist activity' is one that this book sets out to demystify, passing an understanding of the design process back to the end user. This will generate a position from which clients may communicate meaningfully with designers, evaluating their abilities and values, and integrating their vital and valuable professional services into the business of the host organisation.

In their 1997 *Contribution of Design to the UK Economy* report the Design Council recognised the struggle by previous authors and researchers to define design not in terms of profession or specialism but as a socio-economic activity.[1] It identified the following basic approaches:

- Economic/technical: arising from a perspective that attempts to quantify design activity in economic or technical terms.
- Philosophical: arising from a perspective which suggests that design cannot be quantified.
- A synthesis of these two standpoints.

The approach to design taken in this book is a synthesis of the 'economic/technical' and 'philosophical' approaches. Finding the correct balance of these factors on any project determines how successful the outcome will be.

Design often requires resolution of seemingly contradictory thought processes: creativity and logic; innovation and pragmatism; intuition and analysis; listening and talking; problem identification and problem solving; progress and control; technical and strategic thought. It involves reconciliation of aesthetic and sensory qualities with legal and statutory implications.

To articulate intention during the design process requires a range of communication skills – visual awareness, three-dimensional thinking, drawing abilities, verbal communication.

Design must simultaneously add value to a business, express visually its own unique purpose and qualities, and function successfully.

THE DESIGN PROCESS

The design process is not purely linear, but a simplified overview may be described in a linear fashion as shown in Figure 1.1 to permit further discussion of iterative aspects of the process.

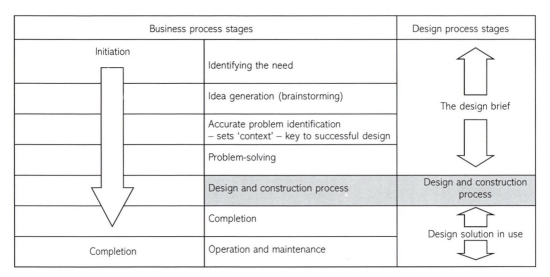

Figure 1.1   The design process from a client organisation's point of view: 'design' is one small part of an overall process

Figure 1.1 outlines the design process in its broadest sense and can be applied to all design disciplines. A business or other need is identified, following which ideas will be proposed for meeting that need. A single idea will be selected from the list of potential ideas and this will be developed to completion and use. The importance of this early stage and its ability to influence all later stages in a positive or negative manner is obvious. It will also be recognised that it applies generically to most forms of business process and indeed other everyday basic human activity. Although the levels of complexity and speed of 'life cycle' are different in each, crossing a busy road and business planning have much in common as processes, each requiring an appropriate 'design' to suit the identified objective in response to external conditions, and each requiring progress and control with constant evaluation and re-evaluation of earlier decisions.

The importance of the client to the success of the overall design process should be apparent from Figure 1.1. The design brief establishes the context of the future actions of all contributors to a design project. While the brief will contain problem-solving guidance relative to the need for the project, the key aspect is the problem identification stage. In design, as with many things in life, the correct answer will only ever emerge in response to the correct question.

While individual projects have a defined timescale, the design process is an iterative process which never truly stops. The reasons for this iteration may be driven by the search for a response to changes from either internal or external influences and constraints. For example, improvements to a design may become apparent in use, from observations regarding materials, function, ergonomics, economics of manufacture and so on, and may represent incremental improvements in the operation and maintenance of a design, the point here being that 'the need', and hence the brief, and the identified demands of the end user remain unchanged. This represents internal influences; the original design context remains largely intact.

Changes to a design may also arise due to external influences and constraints, for example to reflect the changing demands of the end user over time, perhaps in response to the introduction and availability of new technologies and/or materials, or in response to new designs introduced by business competitors. The point here is that the design context has changed. A 'new need' for a design has been identified, and a new design brief and design are required once again to fulfil this need.

It will be understood from this that the design process is substantially aided, in the early stages particularly, by careful and considered analysis of the 'host business' and 'host business resource' issues. The ability to listen, carry out accurate analysis and do so with objective and clear communication is central to success.

The issue of communication is a vital one, for it is not used here as a 'buzzword', but to define meaningful *dialogue* between all contributors and stakeholders involved in the project. This dialogue demands the simultaneous and collective understanding of aims, aspirations, language and process of all project contributors.

It is useful to consider the design process as a collection of activities that share common features, as listed by Freeman:[2]

- Experimental design: broadly defined as exploratory work/prototyping/introduction of new products and processes etc.
- Routine design engineering: broadly defined as the application of known technologies and processes to individual projects
- Fashion design: broadly defined as aesthetic design and styling perhaps, indeed 'often', only considering issues of 'form'
- Design management: defined as the 'planning and coordinating activity necessary to create, make and launch a new product on the market'.

This book suggests that achieving a successful design process demands that all of the above elements must be present and must coexist during the life of the project.

DESIGN DISCIPLINES AND THE DESIGN PROFESSION

The design profession spans a wide range of activities. Definition of the various categories is sure to spark debate amongst designers, as many discipline boundaries are indistinct and many organisations involved in design, large or small, invariably categorise according to their own business needs and market perspective.

The Chartered Society of Designers has 'group contacts' for the following membership categories:

- Graphics
- Interiors
- Exhibitions

- Textiles and Fashion
- Product
- Lifelong Learning Forum.

The Department for Culture, Media and Sport has a broader overview of creative activity generally, and in their *Creative Industries Mapping Document*[3] categorised the following sectors of creative activity to gather and present economic data:

- Advertising
- Architecture
- Arts and antiques market
- Crafts
- Design
- Designer fashion
- Film
- Interactive leisure software
- Music
- Performing arts
- Publishing
- Software
- Television and radio.

The Design Council's *Design in Britain 2000–2001* report (2000) lists the following broad categories of design courses:[4]

- Graphic Communication
- Graphic Design
- Printing Design
- Typography
- Textile Design
- Illustration
- Industrial Design
- Interior Design
- Theatre Design
- Design Management
- Craft, Design and Technology
- Media Design
- Advertising Design
- Design and Heritage
- Photography
- Animation
- Film/Video.

DESIGN AS DISTINCT DISCIPLINES

The types of design activity to be considered in this book will be, in the main, multidisciplinary projects for the built environment. This aligns the book closely with architectural and interior-design-related projects as generic activities, rather than with any specialist area of design in particular. Both of these disciplines intrinsically lead and coordinate multidisciplinary activity, drawing together specialist inputs of many kinds. Broad definitions of design discipline are given in Table 1.1.

Table 1.1   Definitions of design disciplines

Discipline	Overview description
Architecture	From involvement in town planning issues to the design of individual buildings, to involvement with interior design and furniture
Interior design	From architecturally based activity to retail design, commercial design of hotels, leisure design, furniture design etc.
Exhibition design	Museum design, art gallery design, trade stand design, temporary exhibitions, interpretative design, and planning etc.
Graphic design	From corporate identity and strategic marketing, from printed literature to signage, from multimedia interface design to packaging
Product design	From individual craft items to engineering-based mass production products
Multimedia and audio-visual design	Design of computer-based software design and hardware specification
Structural engineering design	Design of structural elements and materials
Mechanical and electrical services design	Design of mechanical and electrical services: electrical power, lighting, heating, ventilation etc.

The philosophy of this book holds strongly to the concept of identifying features common to all areas of design in the same way that it also searches to articulate the aspects of design which are common to other areas of everyday human activity.

THE IMPORTANCE OF DESIGN

The importance of design arises from its functional, commercial and 'added value' contribution to an organisation, but also from its broader and often less tangible cultural, and symbolic contribution and stimuli to society.

Commercial or other added value to an organisation arises from achieving business objectives in a manner that provides competitive advantage. Depending on the

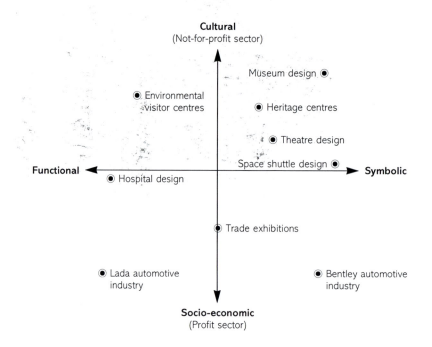

Figure 1.2   Perceptual map locating different design needs

business sector and the strategic objectives of the client organisation, the added value may be achieved by increasing profit or market share, or may be more culturally motivated where an organisation operates in the 'not-for-profit' sector.

However, business and society benefit from good design not only through well-functioning goods produced by the design process but also through being provided with concepts, images, objects, buildings and spaces which deliver intellectual stimuli and important messages about 'the way we do things' and the way we perceive our culture and ourselves. At a basic socioeconomic level, people aspire to own or be associated with goods that project an image they find enhancing in some way. At a more refined level, people gain a sense of well-being from a well-designed, well-functioning interior, or gain new cultural insights about themselves and their heritage

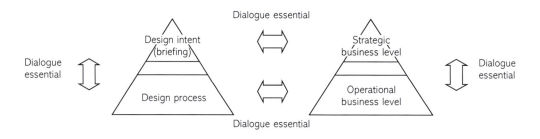

Figure 1.3   Relationship of design to corporate strategy formulation

from intelligently designed interpretative displays in art galleries and museums. Figure 1.2 locates needs for design according to two axes.

Figure 1.3 shows the relationship of design to corporate strategy formulation. Design is not necessarily in itself strategic, being essentially a transformation process, but it is a leading component of corporate strategy formulation. If it has not been proactively considered during the formulation of a corporate strategy it's still 'in there', but on an inadequately structured basis.

Design intent, like the business objectives that define it, is a strategic business issue defined through market analysis. The design strategy is informed by the marketing mix. The design process is an operational level business issue.

The design process is project-based, with individuals contributing to unique one-off products or services. Coordination of these inputs is needed to achieve what is required. The individual contributors are providing sets of distinct capabilities rather than standard services.

Design transforms inputs into outputs using creative and technical skills (see Figure 1.4). It takes in all available 'inputs' or resources – staff, cash, machines, time, and so on – and carries out the necessary transformations to produce outputs or desired objectives, be they physical products, services or information.

Figure 1.4   Inputs to and outputs from the design process

The two – inputs and outputs – must be matched to ensure alignment of initial expectations with the final result, and are both are identified in response to the internal and external business environment.

DESIGN PROJECT MANAGEMENT

Design project management is not simply 'project management' of the objective and quantitative logistics and pragmatics of the production and/or manufacturing stages, although it encompasses these and never loses sight of them. For the purposes of this book, design project management is defined as the holistic and proactive planning, coordination and management of all multidisciplinary ideas and processes involved in progressing a project – from ensuring accurate identification of 'the business need', through all design development and production stages to final use by the client. This includes consideration of maintenance issues and feedback for future projects or business requirements. It places clarity of intent as *the* central element required to ensure controlled progress and optimised creative opportunity (Figure 1.5).

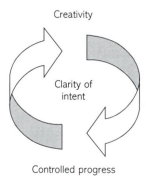

Creativity

Clarity of intent

Controlled progress

Figure 1.5   Centrality of clarity of intent

While traditional project management of the production stages may assume an acceptance of design decisions made by others during the earlier stages of organisational briefing and design briefing, design management drives the entire process by ensuring that qualitative as well as quantitative design concerns are aligned with strategic organisational objectives. This involves iterative questioning and re-evaluation of all stages, involving all team members during the complete life of the project. It involves balanced and simultaneous consideration of strategic, marketing and operational business parameters with the appropriate level of design project parameters.

Successful design project management creates a tangible 'third-party' presence for a project – a 'pulse' perceivable by all design team contributors. The creation of this 'project pulse' is a key point in establishing a 'single vision', and a clarity of purpose for all team members. The requirements of the project to develop and grow to completion are clear to all contributors. There is now a single shared vision and route map: the 'what', 'where' and 'how'.

In leadership and business management theory this process is termed envisioning. Successful design project management provides a synthesis of concern for business outcome and concern for design with the leadership qualities required to achieve the objectives.

THE DESIGN MANAGER

It is clear that to achieve the above synthesis and coordination of inputs requires many qualities, so what makes a design manager?

Design management involves understanding, coordinating and synthesising a wide range of inputs while working alongside a diverse cross-section of multidisciplinary colleagues. Contributors will range from strategic 'board of management' to maintenance operators; from freethinking creative designers to the technically driven; from the aesthetically minded stylist to those driven by the need for compliance with statutory regulation; from those searching for ergonomic efficiency to those demanding financial and market success.

Programme deadlines	⇨ ⇦	Quality
Progress	⇨ ⇦	Control
Pragmatic	⇨ ⇦	Creative
Closure	⇨ ⇦	Exploration
Budget control	⇨ ⇦	Unique design
Economic benefits	⇨ ⇦	Cultural benefits
Function	⇨ ⇦	Aesthetics
Technical	⇨ ⇦	Stylistic
Statutory consents	⇨ ⇦	Innovative solutions
Operational	⇨ ⇦	Strategic
Maintenance	⇨ ⇦	Innovative materials & solutions

Figure 1.6   A 'force-field' diagram

A design manager must therefore bring a range of skills to a project team if success is to be achieved. He/she must be able to understand and communicate in the languages of the many contributors, and must manage the conflicting demands made by balancing controlled progress with support for creative activity and maintaining the programme: to process, understand, reinterpret and coordinate conflicting items of information and conflicting technical, creative, financial and all manner of other demands. The ability to maintain the objective 'project perspective' as the criterion for all decision-making while being bombarded with such diverse data, demanding immediate redistribution and requests for action from all around, requires objective, pragmatic and creative capabilities in addition to intellectual stamina.

The successful design manager is likely to have experience of and/or qualifications in a creative/design background and is likely to combine this with pragmatic sensibilities and experience of and/or qualifications in business studies. Presentation and communication skills and information management skills are other essentials.

The conflicting pressures acting on the project that the design manager must manage can be illustrated using a 'force-field diagram' (Figure 1.6).

DEFINITION OF A SUCCESSFUL DESIGN PROJECT

What do we mean by a successful design project, and can success be measured? Before moving into other more detailed aspects of this book we must consider and define what is meant by success, how it might be measured, and from whose perspective it should be judged.

The best judge of success is the project's client organisation, more specifically the client's financial 'supporters', whether customers and shareholders/trustees or other financial backers. This is true whether the client operates within the profit or not-for-profit sector. The client is the originator of the 'need' and usually, although not always, the provider of the funds required to initiate and carry out the project and to operate in, for, or with the finished design.

If the project adds value to the client's business through additional sales or visits and so on, then the project may be judged a success. This does not necessarily mean, however, that success may be judged only on a commercial basis or determined by increased profit or market share. It may also be judged through cultural or other social gain, in museum or art gallery design, for example, by providing increased access to items of cultural heritage both physically and intellectually and to new audiences, whether younger/older or physically/mentally disabled. If the project is judged to be a success by designers but does not 'add value' in whatever organisational terms apply, then there is an argument that the project cannot truly be judged a success. In these circumstances, it is likely that superficial aesthetic or other narrowly defined aspects of the project are being assessed.

The means of adding value to the business entity, therefore, can only be determined by the client and must be identified or articulated in the brief. This illustrates the importance of the client's role in the design process from the outset. The key is increasing customer benefits, as this in turn produces business gain or 'added value' through increased customer sales/use/visits and so on. A hierarchy of design objectives is illustrated in Figure 1.7.

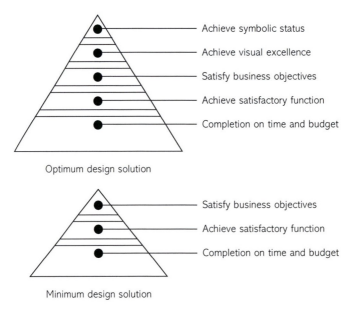

Achieve symbolic status

Achieve visual excellence

Satisfy business objectives

Achieve satisfactory function

Completion on time and budget

Optimum design solution

Satisfy business objectives

Achieve satisfactory function

Completion on time and budget

Minimum design solution

Figure 1.7   Hierarchy of design objectives

THE CLIENT BRIEF

Design does not begin as a personal expression, like some art, although as in any area of human endeavour there is much scope for individual interpretation and unique expression. The success of a design must be assessed in relation to its brief, in addition to any further levels of intuitive subjective response if an objective assessment is to be achieved. It is also clear therefore that one cannot assess the success of a design without an understanding in the first instance of the organisational parameters or project brief underlying the design brief.

The most important factor in carrying out a design project lies not with the designer, but with the client. This is due to the understanding that only the client will have of the business sector and organisational environment in which the design analysis/process is to take place. This is the design context. We noted earlier that only the client, driven by the need to satisfy the demands of shareholders/customers, can identify the key business objectives, whether cultural or commercial, and develop a brief to achieve these objectives. This must incorporate all available resources and other operational issues essential to achieving a successful conclusion to any design project. It may only be the start of the design process but it is the source of the clarity of intent required for all subsequent stages, and the foundation for all subsequent actions.

Any unresolved strategic or operational issues within a design brief will manifest themselves in the finished product as unresolved design issues. Any unresolved client briefing issues will be identified and may be resolved during the design process, but this is wasteful of design time and other project and organisational resources, and may lead to additional costs and/or ill feeling. Clients will also find themselves wading through design proposals that do not exploit business opportunities and meet business objectives.

The key to success therefore lies in ensuring that the brief and all project parameters are clearly articulated, communicated and observed by all contributors from day one. The brief is the central nervous system of successful design.

THE ROLE OF A CLIENT IN A SUCCESSFUL PROJECT

What makes a good client? If it is accepted that a successful design project is one that is judged to be so from the client's perspective and that a clear brief is vital, we must consider what role a client may play in ensuring a successful outcome.

We have already established that the client organisation originates the project through an identified business need, and that the client organisation and their customers/shareholders will also judge success by measuring added value to their business, further purchases, use and so on. This key involvement of the client as initiator, financier, end user and judge of success is self-evident, but the role of client has received little attention in design literature to date. This book aims to fill that gap.

In simplified terms a good client may come from any business sector and must ensure that:

- A clear brief is provided, identifying:
  - business objectives
  - finance
  - programme
  - resources
- A clear internal reporting structure is identified
- A change control mechanism is identified
- An appropriate client design team structure is identified.

While the activity which lies in between the initiation and successful conclusion of a project is mapped out in some detail within this book, a primary aim is to stress the importance of the early organisational briefing and design briefing stages. Equally important is the need to maintain a consistent, objective and honest approach in dealing with project contributors, both within the client organisation and without, to enable the clear definition of project roles and optimum input from all contributors.

NOTES

1. A. Sentence and J. Clarke, *The Contribution of Design to the UK Economy*, London: Design Council, 1997.
2. C. Freeman, 'Design and British Economic Performance' lecture, The Design Centre, London, 23 March 1983.
3. Creative Industries Taskforce, *Creative Industries Mapping Document*, London: Department for Culture, Media and Sport, 1998.
4. Design Council, *Design in Britain 2000–2001*, London: Design Council, 2000.

2 Assembly of the client team

PURPOSE

The purpose of this chapter is to outline the key factors relating to personnel selection which must be considered by any client organisation embarking on a design project. This requires an understanding not only of the professionals outside the client organisation, but also of the professionals who may be appointed from within to complete the design team. This chapter therefore aims to illustrate common areas of business practice and concern shared by clients and designers to help overcome the cultural and operational professional differences that may otherwise lead to conflict.

OUTLINE

- Introduction: assembly of the client design project team
- Aims of a client organisation
- The multidisciplinary nature of a client organisation
- Aims of a design consultancy and their implications for designers
- The client/designer relationship
- Selection of project personnel
- Who is the project for?
- The project director.

INTRODUCTION: ASSEMBLY OF THE CLIENT DESIGN PROJECT TEAM

Assembly of the client organisation project team is a task that must be performed with the greatest of care. Gathering the resources necessary for a project requires a client organisation to identify and commit money, equipment and people. The main difference between these resources is that while the money and equipment inform decisions to be taken, it is the people who take the decisions. While the amount of money available and the capabilities of equipment will be easily quantified and are likely to fulfil the performance expected, it is people that are the variable factor.

It follows therefore that regardless of the sophistication of the technological and financial resources available to a client in support of a project, a key factor, if not *the* key factor in achieving success, rests with the personnel involved. This applies just as much at the operational project level as it does at the board of management level. It applies to the selection of personnel within the client organisation just as much as it applies to the selection of external personnel and consultants. Given the emphasis already placed on the importance of the client's role in a design project, it is suggested that next to preparation of an appropriate brief, the selection of internal client personnel is the most important issue to get right if design project success is to be ensured. Only correctly identifying the strategic project objectives carries equal significance at this most fundamental level.

Many of these decisions will be taken before the appointment of designers and other project personnel. This chapter therefore considers the importance that the selection of client personnel has for a project. It examines the effect that the differing professional backgrounds and perspectives that various contributors bring to a project has on the personnel project dynamic, and establishes how to coordinate the arising multiplicity of views into a single coherent 'client-focused voice'. It considers the selection of the client project director, the role required to coordinate those views from the organisation's perspective overall.

Although there will be many technical and functional contributors to a project from a wide variety of professional disciplines as noted above, the two key business perspectives to be considered are those of 'the client' and 'the designer'. The nature of the relationship that is created and exists between the two during the project is briefly explored. Like any relationship in or out of business, it requires to be worked at to succeed and needs mutual understanding and respect if that success is to be sustained and optimised.

Before examining the issues relating to the selection of individual personnel for the project, we must therefore first consider the aims and the motivations of client organisations and of designers individually on a broad and general level for two reasons:

- to enable us to understand the similar areas of motivation underlying designers and their clients. This book will continue to emphasise the broader similarities while discussing the more obvious literal differences between clients and designers;
- to illustrate why the specific operational and cultural business concerns of the client must be *explicitly* built into a design brief.

AIMS OF A CLIENT ORGANISATION

Strategic

The strategic business aims of clients and hence the motivations for any design project being planned vary enormously, depending on a range of issues, for example the nature of the host industry, and the shape and size of the organisation. In particular, the source and nature of the funding of an organisation and the financial return demanded by the owners of a business, whether shareholders or trustees and so on, will determine the objectives. Businesses commissioning design projects range in size and organisational complexity from sole traders on the one hand to global conglomerates and governmental organisations on the other. For commercially driven business organisations the quest to maximise the market value of the company will provide the most explicitly tangible motivation, while for other organisations more cultural ambitions will be the objective. The business aims, however, will always be a mixture of the following financial and non-financial business objectives and professional aspirations:

- Maximisation of revenue income (turnover)
- Maximisation of profit
- Maximisation of growth (one, several or all of the following: growth through increased market share; geographical growth; share value; number of employees; number of products; number of brands and so on)
- Minimising levels of business debt (improving gearing)
- Maximisation of dividend payments
- Community aims (employee benefits and care, managers' welfare, customer/supplier relationships and so on)
- Cultural and environmental aims (arts, heritage, minorities, research, education, ecological aims, environmental aims, business ethics and so on)
- Operational efficiencies
- Marketing and promotional aims (strengthening brands, raising awareness of new products and so on)
- Personal aspirations of managers/directors
- Improved provision of effective services (energy providers, local authorities, NHS and so on).

The motivation for a design project arises directly from the mix of business objectives of a client organisation. Depending on the scale of the project relative to the scale of the core business operation, it will form either some new small part or an all-consuming part in achieving the strategic corporate goals.

Any balance of business objectives is dynamic, not static, and will be influenced by both the external market demands of the business environment, and the internal aspirations of management. In addition to determining the project aims, the mix of the business objectives constitutes a major factor in determining the methods and processes which must be observed during the life of any design project 'hosted' by the organisation. It is only through an understanding of the way in which individual businesses go about achieving their aims ('the way we do things around here') that enables a designer to engage fully with the mechanisms and personality of the host organisation.

Operational

The operational parameters of the client organisation must be fully understood by a designer during the design process. While this will be obvious to most readers from any client organisation, the ability to recognise these parameters and to articulate them formally in writing as part of a brief will not always be so straightforward. Some organisations may also consider that it is part of the designer's task to identify these parameters as part of their design analysis. This 'hands-off' approach is leaving too much to chance and lacks the clarity of foresight that is required at all stages of a project.

A client must gauge the effect that a design project will have upon its organisation at an operational level. The operational methods of an organisation often include many unwritten, unspoken and perhaps even unrecognised methods and values that arise from its organisational culture. Working successfully with personnel from outside the client organisation requires that the new personnel be briefed on those 'organisational norms' if expectations and aspirations are to be shared. In order that appropriate methodologies may be explicitly articulated by the client within the design brief, several broad aspects of operational issues should be borne in mind:

- *Organisational culture and behaviour.* There are many excellent books written entirely about this complex subject. Organisational culture and behaviour are determined by many external and internal factors – business sector, customers, business objectives, management style and structure, language, dress, reward and incentive systems and so on. We are concerned here with ensuring that the explicit and implicit aspects of the organisation's culture and behaviour are understood, and that the design project methodology is aligned with these 'norms'. The effect of the project on staff who will be working on or affected by the project at a peripheral level as well as those more directly affected during the life of the project or involved in the operation of the new entity upon completion must be examined. Their response to the demands of the project should be understood and appropriate measures explicitly established for staff and consultants alike to work to. The onus must rest with the client to establish such a framework.
- *Understanding and communication between professional disciplines.* At the root of the ability to achieve a coordinated project team lies the ability to establish effective communication between professional disciplines and functional organisational disciplines (finance sales IT, estates and so on). This is true within the client's own organisation, critically between key client functions, but is also true within the wider project team, which includes external consultants.

Collectively the mix of these parameters will make the project process unique to each individual client. When properly identified and appropriately managed they will provide unique creative opportunities for the design solution, simultaneously and seamlessly integrating it with the operation of the host business. An understanding of these client organisation business parameters therefore underpins any project design brief and must be explicitly articulated for the designer if the design process is to be successful. The design process itself must be designed for each new design project.

THE MULTIDISCIPLINARY NATURE OF A CLIENT ORGANISATION

Although this book stresses the similarities between clients and designers there are two important areas of distinct difference which it is of value to take note of. These are noted generically and refer particularly to large corporate or government organisations.

One area arises from the differing breadth of professional activities which clients and designers undertake in discharging their core function. Clients often employ a wide range of professionals who each play a part in the overall organisation but each of whom may not be entirely aware of the big picture in an objective manner. Examples might be the National Health Service or a university. Most design practices, even where these are multidisciplinary, are smaller, perhaps driven and influenced by key charismatic individuals and have more shared values and easier internal communications.

Another important difference arises from the project-based reasoning of designers in contrast to the 'ongoing professional bureaucracy' processes demanded of many large client organisations. The effect of these key differences is explored further in the next section.

AIMS OF A DESIGN CONSULTANCY AND THEIR IMPLICATIONS FOR DESIGNERS

The aims and motivations of a design consultancy, like any 'client's business', will consist of a mixture of the previously noted business objectives. In this respect, then, at the strategic level designers are no different from any other business. The way designers go about achieving these aims is also due to the professional and cultural influences particular to their industry, just like any other business organisation. However, while reinforcing these underlying broad similarities, it is useful to be aware of the cultural and industry-specific differences, even in a generalised way at this stage.

Beyond the obvious financial and strategic aims of a design consultancy lie specific motivators and influences with which a client may be unfamiliar. If not understood and managed, these motivators may be a source of poor communication, leading to the risk of misunderstanding, frustration and wasteful debates over the control, direction and scope of the project.

Despite the risk of over-generalising, it is possible to identify some generic areas that will provide an insight into the motivations and thought processes of designers.

- The nature of a designer's workload
- The nature of design education and training
- Creative nature of design personnel.

Workload

Designers by definition work on a series of continual 'one-off' projects, all of varying duration and scope, and all usually, although not always, for a range of client types. Design projects may vary from the fast, 'stand-alone' design of small items of furniture or display to long-term design projects involving marketing, ergonomic or other research, on innovative and or large-scale projects such as new corporate headquarters, new product design and so on. Designers are therefore used to continually forming new professional relationships with ever-changing client groups and with other professionals, each new project group having its own group dynamics and culture as well as its project-specific objectives. This type of workload means that designers have developed strong abilities to focus on project-specific objectives. It can also, although not always, mean that designers develop an awareness of how best to operate alongside a variety of other professional disciplines and personalities in an environment supportive of and sympathetic to the open exchange of ideas and information.

Education and training

Given that the nature of professional training and the subsequent personal aspiration to impress one's professional peers to some extent informs the actions of most ambitious professionals, the nature of a designer's education and training is another area worthy of consideration to provide some insight into their methodologies and their motivations. It should be noted that a design education is distinct from an art education. Design education does not deal purely with aesthetics, but with the origination of objects: buildings, interiors, leaflets, textiles and so on are all required for a particular purpose, and must all be created with an appropriate set of aesthetic qualities using appropriate production technologies.

Although the function, aesthetics and production of an item of design can be philosophically separated and discussed, it is only the successful and seamless fusion of these parameters that make for a successful design. The initial response when asked to pass an opinion on any design should be 'What was the brief?'

The diversity of design disciplines that make up the design industry has already been noted. As might be expected, in design as in any other profession, there is a multitude of approaches to the training of each discipline. Within each discipline there are conflicting points of view regarding key industry issues, even at a fundamental level such as determination of the boundaries of each discipline – for example where does architecture finish and interior design start? Where does textile design finish and fashion design begin?

Broadly speaking, design training for designers of all disciplines sets out to equip them with a personal design philosophy. For three-dimensional designers, this means achieving a design solution whose form and aesthetic qualities arise philosophically from the function of the object/building/interior and the materials and technologies from which it is to be fabricated and the age in which it is being constructed. Many non-designers will be aware of the stereotypical 'Form follows function' and 'Firmness, commodity and delight' designer ideologies.

If this ideological/philosophical approach is maintained at all stages of the design process to develop all the detailed design decisions in addition to providing the initial design strategy and concept, then the design solution will achieve an integrity beyond simple visual success. For example, the visual expression of a building's function will arise from a form that heightens its purpose or typology, so that when designing a cinema, the question is how is the 'cinema experience' defined and how can this experience be heightened?

As stated before, the materials and technologies employed for the construction should be appropriate for the project – reflecting the nature of use of the building and for the age and location within which the project is undertaken. Literal examples of this include contemporary architecture, where the structural and services methods employed in a building are expressed visually so that the function of these elements may be 'read' and understood. For an object the same may also apply: for example the Dyson vacuum cleaner expresses both its working methodology and the materials employed in its construction. In a business context this clear expression and continuity/consistency of intent provides a marketing platform which differentiates through design integrity. In addition to the Dyson product range, the Apple Macintosh range of computers is a further example, having its own operating system in addition to distinct visual product/industrial design. BMW cars – ultimate driving machines – is another. In all cases consistently applied design integrity, not just 'styling', provides competitive advantage through differentiation.

Another important aspect of design education for clients to be aware of relates to the breadth of activity that is felt by each discipline to constitute the design process. Perhaps the longest-established design profession, certainly the best recognised, is that of the architect. Architectural training in particular takes a very broad and methodical view that the design process comprises activities which are concerned on the one hand with conceptual and aesthetic and production design information, and on the other hand with the management and coordination of the many inputs of all design project contributors, at all stages of the process and including the client. It does not, however, investigate or deal with the complexities which may underlie the client business operation, particularly where these complexities compromise the designer's intellectual design philosophy. However, not all design training embraces this breadth of issues, or perhaps even places a value on these wider design management issues.

While it is of course correct and essential that boundaries of professional training and responsibility exist and are defined, the issue of real importance is that these boundaries, and the expectations of all parties involved in a project are simultaneously in alignment. Obviously these expectations and responsibilities must also include all the required design project issues.

Creative nature of designers

The final aspect of a designer's 'psychological make-up' that will be considered here relates to the original reason that designers will have entered the profession. This factor perhaps more than any other will determine the qualities that a designer will bring to a designer/client relationship – the need to create.

While a major motivation for a designer is 'the need to create', this need is shaped by many personal qualities, skills and abilities. Designers, like everyone else, possess artistic, creative and practical skills, mixing intuitive and analytical approaches and linear and iterative processes in a search for originality. Generally designers will use these skills and abilities in a manner that is shaped by their personal ambition, ego, intelligence and general awareness.

The mix of these skills will obviously vary from individual to individual; however, if an intelligent approach to designing is taken, the mix should in a very subtle way also vary during the design process, with a differing skill taking the lead role in synthesising the thought process depending on the perspective and output required at each stage (Figure 2.1).

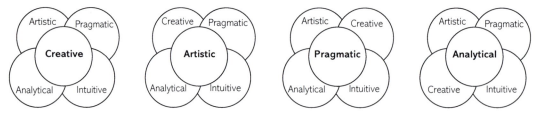

Figure 2.1   Different skills take the lead as appropriate

The skills will be shuffled around, with a new skill taking the lead in turn so that the problem may be viewed from a variety of perspectives. This will continue until a new and unique design solution is formed which is both holistic and bespoke to the individual business and design problem.

Creative skill

Creativity is by no means the exclusive realm of the designer. All businesses start, develop and grow through creativity. However, creativity in any field requires instinct and knowledge. Knowledge may be gained through experience, while instinct is a different matter. A designer will apply their creativity in the context of a design solution to a business problem – a brief – and will synthesise a design solution accordingly.

Artistic skill

Artistic skill is deliberately identified here as separate from creative ability. It is perhaps in this area that many clients will feel themselves to be distant from the abilities of their designers and may often be unwilling or unable to engage in dialogue relating to visual criteria. The level of artistic input required will vary depending on the business sector. Depending on the design discipline, this skill set will influence the look and feel of the solution, involving stylistic, fashion, and surface aesthetics issues generally.

Pragmatic skill

Practical skills and the understanding of technical issues – knowledge of manufacturing/construction/production materials, processes and techniques, knowledge of relevant legislation, and so on – are essential if a design concept is to be successfully turned into a unique physical reality. Where practical and technical skills are weak in a designer, the skills of other contractor/manufacturers are often relied on to complete the design process. Such designers are not designers in the truest sense being closer to 'stylists'. Originality is also likely to be lacking with such an approach since there is a deliberate fragmentation of the design thought process.

Analytical skill

Closely linked to pragmatic skill, this skill set takes designers into areas of management inherent in all aspects of a project – from defining the brief, through considering design options, to project management of the construction/manufacturing process. Analytical skills, however, require both linear 'logic' and lateral 'intuitive' thought processes. Problem identification, problem-solving, physical planning, compliance with statutory requirements, cost–benefit option appraisal and so on will all be involved and must be synthesised appropriately with the artistic and creative solutions and opportunities. The intuitive analytical skills of perceptive and subjective thinking will, to a large extent, determine the degree of 'uniqueness' that will be brought to a final design solution.

Intelligence, ego, general awareness and personal ambition are the final key qualities that will define the approach taken by a designer in synthesising the previously noted design skill sets, and will determine the client/designer relationship to a very large degree. This is no different from any other business relationship, but it does emphasise the benefit of including an assessment of the likely personal 'teamworking dynamic' within the criteria for selection of a designer.

THE CLIENT/DESIGNER RELATIONSHIP

The client/designer relationship is complex and dynamic and depends to a large degree on the nature of the client organisation hosting the design project. The designer may operate at some distance intellectually from a client – simply facilitating technical matters, for example when designing a speculative industrial unit for a developer. A designer may also interact at close quarters and at an intellectual level with a client when designing interpretative displays for museums or galleries, or other design concepts which of necessity include detailed client operational factors, such as a night club concept or themed restaurants/bars. Where there are overlapping areas of intellectual input the process will need particularly sensitive management to ensure controlled progress.

A design project forms a temporary union between a client's business organisation and a design practice organisation. This temporary union has both shared qualities and unique 'stand-alone' qualities (Figure 2.2); however, recognition of this doesn't on its own provide any sense of a new-found unifying direction or project vision.

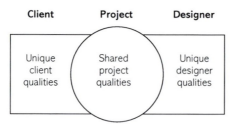

Figure 2.2   A temporary union for a design project

A project vision starts with the business vision in search of a sympathetic and supportive design vision, and must successfully secure a design team that can synthesise the design and business requirements into a single project vision. This project vision is the single direction that unifies all project team inputs (Figure 2.3).

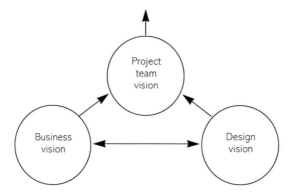

Figure 2.3   Project team vision and direction

Where client organisations of any kind work on an ongoing basis with designers, it will also be apparent that the range of services provided by design practices varies dramatically, with some being stronger in some areas of the design process than in others. Some are strong in conceptual areas of design, some in technical detailing and management; some are strong in all areas. Some do not acknowledge essential parts of the design process as being their responsibility, whereas some, particularly those with an architectural background, are generally stronger in aspects of management and technical ability.

Client organisations should be aware of this range of differing expectations which designers have about 'what design is', and should query carefully during interview stages. This issue is discussed in more detail later in the book.

SELECTION OF PROJECT PERSONNEL

Having broadly considered the aims and motivations of client organisations and design consultants and the relationship that will be created between them, it is time to move on to give further consideration to the selection of suitable project personnel. As noted earlier in the book, this selection is divided into selection of internal client staff personnel and that of personnel from outside the client organisation. Since internal client personnel will be responsible for writing the business brief and making future decisions regarding the selection of future key contributors, the selection of the client's internal project team is described first.

Client's internal project team

The scale of a design project relative to the scale of the client's business operation plays a major part in determining the client's initial actions. A design project may be a one-off project which affects the host organisation very little until it becomes an operational matter upon completion, say a new supermarket for a large chain of stores or a new permanent gallery within a large host museum. Alternatively, the project may consume almost the entire resources of an organisation during its lifetime – a small theatre company building a major new 'home' theatre, for example.

It is therefore clear that the process of selecting personnel may be a simple question of using everyone/whoever is available, or it may be a matter of selecting the most suitable personnel for the project while ensuring that the core business operation continues unaffected. It may require finding and appointing new staff specifically for the purpose. In this book it is assumed that a project is to take place within a large client organisation.

Selecting personnel from within the organisation carries many implications for a client, relating both to the ongoing 'core business' needs, and to the needs of 'the project'. Key issues to bear in mind include the following.

Core business issues

- Can staff be freed from existing organisational priorities and duties? The client organisation must state honestly when appointing an individual to the project that other existing duties and priorities can be reduced and/or revised even where the member of staff is mostly 'project based' and is continually moving from one project to another. A frequent mistake is having unrealistic expectations of continuing all normal duties alongside project duties.
- What changes are required to existing line management structures, (a) to support project staff and (b) to ensure continuity of ongoing core tasks?
- What, if any, additional personnel resources are required to support non-project activities?

Project issues

- What role does the member of staff play in the project?
- What level of authority should the member of staff have in the project structure?
- Do staff have an adequate level of legitimate authority within the organisation to support the project role?

Personal qualities

- Are staff suitably qualified academically?
- Are staff suitably qualified professionally?
  - Do staff have suitable experience?
  - Previous direct experience?
  - Previous related and transferable experience?
- Do staff have suitable personal qualities?
- Do staff have adequate knowledge of the workings of the entire organisation?
  - Reporting to the board of management?
  - Interrelationships of departments?
  - Operational concerns of individual departments?

As noted earlier, since a range of internal client personnel will have to provide inputs to the project, it is also clear that an internal structure must be formed to control and coordinate the views of the client at all stages of the project.

This internal project structure is important for many reasons, a primary one being that it will have a direct influence on the communications of the client organisation internally and with all other external project consultants. A new dynamic will be required of this group which responds to events at the pace required by the project while also acknowledging the pace of the organisation, which is likely to have differing priorities and parameters. Figure 2.4 illustrates the various interrelated factors that exert interacting forces on the project team.

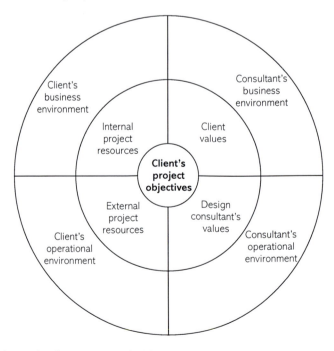

Figure 2.4   The interacting forces on a project team

For this reason, a clear management hierarchy with formal lines of communication must be established from an early date, with the appointments starting 'at the top' with a project director or sponsor. A newsletter or other staff communiqué should be issued at an early date, noting the appointment and the key hierarchical staff positions, even where precise personnel have yet to be interviewed/appointed. This will send a clear signal throughout the organisation that the project process is under way and that the project already has an identifiable structure, character and relationship with the client organisation.

WHO IS THE PROJECT FOR?

In any project there is a range of client stakeholders and hence perspectives. These arise from both the immediate internal environment and the wider business environment. Shareholders, directors, partners, managers, customers, trustees, ministers, local government agencies, local government officers and many others all have an interest in or a contribution to make in one form or another. In the immediate management environment the variety of perspectives arises from a variety of sources of business function: sales, marketing, production, finance, maintenance, personnel, political, economic, technical, social, environmental.

It is clear that the aims of a project will follow on from the strategic business objectives of the client, but although this is logically irrefutable, there is no guarantee that the personnel who are given project responsibilities will keep it in mind.

Experience of project-based work often shows that individuals appointed to provide specialist inputs to a project will not always fully understand the specific project aims, or indeed the strategic business aims. Individual aspirations and/or the desire to optimise the aims of individual departments can, if they remain unchecked, render the project process suboptimal. This will often happen through misguided best intentions, although also through attempts to place the achievement of personal recognition above the collective project objectives.

Such a problem is likely to be more serious the larger and more complex an organisation becomes, and is likely to be particularly true of not-for-profit organisations, given the lack of a unifying profit motive. All design team members have specific areas of expertise to contribute: marketing, scientific, engineering, curatorial, academic, IT, financial, estates and design. Each discipline may be biased towards the optimisation of its own particular professional interest. This intensity of spirited individual contributions is a necessary and desirable thing, and should ensure that the project benefits from an enterprising and fluent expression of multidisciplinary professional concerns if managed appropriately. However, a balance of professional viewpoints must be reached which optimises the project vision priorities. This requires excellence in management, coordination and often negotiation skills, and brings us to consider the establishment of a single coordinating role within the client organisation and the importance of such a role for the entire project.

THE PROJECT DIRECTOR

The appointment of a project director, often termed a project sponsor, together with the early establishment of a formal hierarchical structure of project authority and lines of communication for reporting progress and other issues back to the board of management, are key aspects of a client's capacity to coordinate its particular variety of professional/functional inputs required for a design project.

This coordinating role may be carried out by someone from within or outside the client organisation. Whoever is chosen, it must be someone with a clear understanding of the host business and its organisational structure, the project objectives and the available project resources. They must also be aware of the requirements of objectively progressing a project and all the conflicting demands and priorities that this entails. They must be formally given, and recognised by all project contributors and all personnel within the client organisation as having, the power that the legitimate authority of project director brings.

This is quite distinct from acknowledging other informal routes of communication, and indeed influence, that may exist elsewhere within the client organisation and that may affect the project in some way.

The role, responsibilities and powers of the project director, like the roles of all design team members, must be clearly determined. The issue of most importance for the client, however, is that of identifying the correct person to carry out the correct role, and establishing the correct degree of legitimate autonomy which the role requires to fulfil the brief.

Selection and role

The project director must:

- understand the objectives of the project and its capacity to add value to the client's business;
- understand the underlying processes, culture and values of the client;
- understand the underlying processes, culture and values of the design consultant;
- understand and empathise with the design project process;
- have an understanding of contract and employment law.

The person chosen for the role must command the respect of other senior client organisation contributors. This respect will be earned only through the ability to make prompt, well-informed, consistent and honest decisions at all stages of the project.

The role of the project director is to make the overall aims of the project the focus of his/her effort in the context of optimising the ongoing business concerns of the organisation. This role requires strong, objectively formed leadership and management skills, with the ability to question, to judge and to maintain an objective and clear overview while receiving a multitude of conflicting information relating to the project and operational business and strategic issues. The project director must be in a position to deal effectively with all constituent client and other project contributors, and to analyse objectively all individual comments and requests, and to negotiate and clarify subjective issues. This must all be achieved in a positive and non-confrontational manner. The project director must evaluate the range of options, and press contributors for still further options that might maximise the client's business aims from the project.

A non-confrontational but assertive approach is essential in questioning and drawing forth the views of contributors, many of which will be passionately held. Gaining the respect and cooperation of all team members is vital. Leadership skills and a balance of right-brain and left-brain thinking, that is, of creative and linear rational thinking, are required, as the project director must balance the key elements of progress versus control, continually trading off on the one hand 'hard issues', such as cost and programme, each of which will be largely predetermined, against 'soft issues', such as creative opportunity and development of ideas and, indeed, changes of direction. A 'balanced-brain' personality is less likely to hold extreme views, but will generally see the strengths of a range of views and will play devil's advocate with great diplomacy. To illustrate the middle ground of balanced-brain thinking, the extremes can be listed as follows:

Left brain *(hard)*	*Right brain* *(soft)*
Logical	Artistic
Serious	Humorous
Rational	Psychic
Planner	Improviser
Sequential	Intuitive
Systematic	Emotional
Punctuality	Lateness
Objective	Subjective
Linear	Playful
Pragmatic	Creative
Single-minded	Vague

The project director's leadership and management process

Above all else, the project director must provide clarity and direction to all project contributors. This means establishing a formal management hierarchy and lines of communication. However, leadership and management of the design project process require recognition not only of the essential formal and explicit processes but also of informal and often invisible processes that contributors will inevitably utilise. The project in effect forms a temporary mini political system for the project team.

Recognition of the three models of social management mechanism put forward by Maidment and Thomson[1] for the coordination of political and socioeconomic activity goes some way towards understanding the variety of coordinating processes that will take place during the life of the project. The three models are Hierarchies, Networks and Markets.

- **Hierarchy**: a structural mechanism for bringing about coordination in running a large and complex organisation, or making a large number of individuals act together for a collective purpose. A task or policy or project is progressively broken down into discrete elements that are entrusted to individuals to carry out or supervise. The overall process is factored into a number of sub-processes that collectively make up the original objective. Key features of a hierarchy are 'rules, authority, administration, superordination, subordination'.
- **Network**: a 'flat organisational form' including 'equality of membership', most often deployed where a set of professionals such as legal, medical, architectural and accountancy form the network, and tend to organise and regulate themselves in a close and often closed network context. Key features of a network are informality, solidarity (by common/shared experience), trust (the central organising feature), loyalty, but also elitism and exclusion of outsiders.
- **Markets**: a market is a mechanism by which buyers and sellers meet to trade for goods or services for a price, with money being exchanged (rather than by barter). All markets are interrelated and it is because of these links that markets serve to coordinate a vast range of human activity. Key features of a market are price, supply, demand, self-interest, competition and formal contracts. The central coordinating factor is price.

During a project all three mechanisms are present to varying degrees at various points, depending on what is happening, what is required and who is involved.

To assist in managing these factors the project director must prepare and distribute a regular status report on all key areas of the project development in a standard format. The report should aim to be concise and to communicate key concerns and areas of progress. It is a summary of all that is important in relation to the project, not a detailed analysis. It has at least two audiences to reach:

- Those outside the project team. This includes the client organisation board of management and all staff, who should be able to obtain a rapid, concise and accurate status report
- Those within the project team. It should provide them with an opportunity to stand back and assess their own input from an overview perspective.

The project director's report should be structured as follows, with each of the component parts being supplied by the relevant key contributors and rewritten in the project director's own style:

- Executive summary
- Progress report overall (narrative)

- Client report (narrative)
- Design team report (narrative)
- Contractor's report (narrative)
- Financial report and forecast
- Programme and forecast
- Circulation list.

While simple, jargon-free language is essential, the use of photographs and diagrams to make key points will provide an immediate and beneficial sense of 'where things are'.

In addition to circulating the project director's report to all contributors and throughout the client organisation, it is important that progress is reported honestly and in a consistent manner if project contributors and other non-project staff are to continue to support the venture. Reports are dealt with in more detail in Chapters 4 and 7.

NOTE

1. Richard Maidment and Grahame Thomson (eds), *Managing the United Kingdom*, London: Sage Publications, 1993.

3   The briefing process

PURPOSE

The purpose of this chapter is to outline the briefing process and emphasise its importance in relation to the entire design project process.

The briefing structure given within this chapter sets out to illustrate a layered, prioritised and logical sequence of information clarification that continually empowers and unites all new design project contributors through seeking progressive contributions at each level of briefing as the process is progressed. In addition to setting up the creative brief, the design briefing process described permits client organisations to obtain comparative design concepts from selected design practices/teams, and undertake an objective design proposal evaluation process which will become a bespoke and integrated element of the contractual document prepared for the appointed design consultant.

OUTLINE

- Introduction
- Importance of the brief
- The briefing process.

INTRODUCTION

It is clear that the brief provides a central body of information that all contributors will use to focus and coordinate their activities. Preparation of the client design brief is a particularly interesting stage because it is the first point at which an attempt is made to link the internally generated new business idea with external personnel and with the organisation's own ongoing business requirements. It is therefore a task that should not be underestimated. It should not be assumed that if a simple brief is prepared by the client, the professionals – the consultants – will sort everything else out at a later date. In fact this approach is a recipe for disaster – for everyone.

However, while the preparation of the various briefing documents required during the briefing process has several important stages, all stages of briefing, and not just the early stages of identifying business objectives, are proactively managed by the client organisation.

IMPORTANCE OF THE BRIEF

The importance of the briefing process to a project arises from the fact that it simultaneously provides project controls and presents creative opportunity. Properly written, a design brief will:

- Define the project objectives
- Define the specific business opportunity that must be realised through meeting the project objectives
- Define the scope for creative opportunity from the design team
- Facilitate control over the final outcome of a design project for both clients and designers by articulating the new business idea, the operational business framework within which the idea must be achieved, and the financial and non-financial resources that are available.

The capacity of the brief to facilitate control while defining creative and business opportunity applies not only during the pre-project setting-up process, but also during the project running stage and the post-completion stage. It will become clear that the briefing process links all parts of the design project process, from 'business idea' to completed 'operational business concern'. It also creates the device that links client personnel with other project consultants and is therefore a central coordinating project mechanism. The project is represented in its earliest most tangible form within the design brief, which is the earliest point at which the project, as an intention, conceptually leaves the parameters of internal client organisation discussion.

The briefing process provides controls and opportunities at the following stages of the project.

General: at all stages

- Control: it provides a focus for all contributors
- Control: it identifies specific qualitative targets to be achieved by the project
- Control: it identifies specific quantitative targets to be achieved by the client
- Control: it makes the business concept tangible.

Pre-project

- Opportunity: linked with a suitable interview process, it provides an objective basis for exploring and selecting suitable design concepts and consultants
- Opportunity and control: it provides the client with the means of defining the level of creative input, that is, the level of conceptual design required
- Control: it provides key project parameters – time, budget and resources
- Control: it provides the basis of contractual agreements between the client and the consultants.

During the project

- Control: it provides a guide to decision-taking where a compromise between conflicting priorities must be resolved and agreed
- Opportunity: it establishes the creative and business context by setting out the design criteria that must be satisfied – the client organisation 'what', and the identified design team 'how'.

Post-project

- Control: it provides the key information for assessing the level of success of the project – That is, does the reality match the concept?
- Control: it provides the key information for assessing the level of success of contributors to the project
- Opportunity: it provides information on the performance of project contributors to inform decisions for future projects through objective analysis of data
- Opportunity: it provides information on the financial and programme parameters of a project to inform decisions for future projects through objective analysis of data.

THE BRIEFING PROCESS

The overall briefing process has several identifiable stages that are described in this chapter.

Briefing spans the entire project process in various forms, from the strategic corporate planning stage to the post-project evaluation stage, but is at its most proactive and formal stages before the appointment of a design team and during the preparation of the client design brief. The purpose of the client design brief is to permit

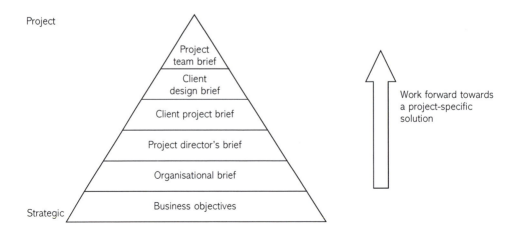

Figure 3.1   Hierarchy of briefing stages from a business perspective

a suitable design team to be identified and appointed by issuing the client design brief as an 'invitation to tender' document to selected design practices. The hierarchy of briefing stages can be illustrated as in Figure 3.1.

The stages are expanded on in what follows.

Business objectives

Any design project starts its life as a business need identified by a client organisation as part of its ongoing strategic corporate planning process. The need may arise from an ongoing programme of refurbishment/renewal or may arise from planned business growth/expansion or diversification and so on. The objective of the project is to fulfil part of the ongoing vision for the organisation. The relationship of business vision, mission statement and business objectives is shown in Figure 3.2.

Figure 3.2   A business hierarchy

Organisational brief (a board of management document)

From the organisational business need identified during the strategic corporate planning process, key organisational parameters are established and approved by the board of management. They will include major project determining factors such as budget, timescale, and available resources. The organisational brief will also include initial thoughts on leadership and management of the project, albeit perhaps only in principle. Using the organisational brief, the board of management will interview and appoint a project director.

Before assembling the project design team and writing the client design brief, the client organisation must be in a position to write an organisational brief for the project director. The production of a formal organisational statement identifying the strategic project aims and objectives at the earliest possible stage will prove an invaluable source of focus for identifying all key decisions to follow, at all stages of the project. This statement of project objectives is a key component of the design brief. The organisational brief is the foundation of all future briefing documents and hence project actions.

The organisational brief must articulate the following strategic issues:

- Key project objectives:
  - What are the aims of the project? Business aims, creative aims, cultural aims, social aims, financial aims, and so on.

- Key organisational business parameters:
  - When must the project be completed?
  - What resources can be/must be made available? Finance, personnel, equipment/ plant and so on.
  - What other important factors exist? Requirements of funding bodies, return on capital, ongoing business concerns, that is, phased works, integration with existing work and so on, reporting and approval process, involvement of the board of management and so on.
- Key operational parameters of the organisation:
  - Ongoing operational processes and requirements
  - Schedule of critical project accommodation, equipment and so on
  - Reporting parameters
  - Cultural parameters.

No knowledge of design or project-specific experience is needed to identify these issues. They are business issues with which all client organisations will be familiar, and the link to the corporate planning process is clear. They do require coordinated agreement within the client organisation.

Verification of the organisational brief at board of management level will enable development of a brief for the project director. Gaining this verification will probably require a coordinated series of cost–benefit analysis at board of management level. This brief may be anything from two pages to a detailed report, but whatever format is established it must be formally acknowledged and approved by the client organisation.

Project director's brief

The project director's brief will include general guidance for the project director setting out the broad parameters within which the project may be developed but also specific strategic and non-negotiable parameters. Where the project director is appointed from within the organisation there is a danger that the brief will be minimal, in the belief that familiarity and experience make full details unnecessary. Such an informal approach is not recommended. Where a project director is appointed from outside the existing organisation a more detailed and formal brief will certainly be required.

Although carrying out the role of project director requires very particular personal qualities and experience, as already noted, it cannot be done without clearly established and formally approved project parameters to permit the relative value of conflicting project factors to be objectively and consistently assessed. The project director's brief is as important for other contributors as it is for the project director, as it provides a clear basis for evaluating objectivity and continuity in the project director's decision-making. With this consistency and clarity a shared project vision becomes possible.

The brief required by the project director is one of the most fundamental aspects of any project. It is a development of the organisational brief, and it is from this brief that all other briefing documents of a project are built. Any unresolved issues here will reverberate throughout the life of the project and into the finished product, wasting time, effort, resources and opportunity, and frustrating contributors at all turns.

The project director's brief must determine fundamental issues:

- What is the key role of the project director and what are the key reporting and approval processes?
- How does the project fit with the strategic business plan?
  - At a strategic level?
  - At a marketing level?
  - At an operational level?
- Is the project one-off or part of a continuing programme?
- How are other core business activities affected during the duration of the project?
- What are the approved organisational resources?
  - Finance (capital)
  - Finance (revenue)
  - Personnel
  - Machines and plant
- What are the critical project issues and outcomes?
  - Timescale
  - Quality
  - Return on finance
  - Low operational costs and so on.

For example, a one-off capital project to build and fit out a new furniture manufacturing factory unit for a 'local employer' will place differing demands on a project director from the construction and fitting out of a new high profile airport terminal, not only in terms of scale, but also in terms of organisational priorities. The local employer is likely to place most emphasis on completion on time and to cost, particularly if increased production is required to meet a specific customer order. The airport terminal project director, while still expected to meet a deadline to an agreed cost, will also be expected to deliver a building and interior which provide a symbol of national importance with innovative, often untried, aspects of customer service at the point of delivery.

Client project brief

The client project brief is likely to be the first formal project document prepared by the project director. In addition to the information contained in the organisational brief prepared by the board of management, it will include the project director's methodology for delivering the project. This may include the appointment of key staff and significant 'milestones' to be achieved during the overall timescale. It will also outline the formally approved business relationship between the project and the ongoing core concern of the organisation, and enable the internal project team to prepare the client design brief.

For example, the client project brief prepared by the project director for a new permanent gallery within an existing museum may identify the requirement for staff resources of (say) three curators (from two different departments) three or more conservators, one education officer, two in-house designers (part-time only), two or more in-house multimedia designers and so on. The client project brief provides these contributors and their line managers with clear parameters for dividing their time between core duties and project duties by providing verification of the organisation's legitimate commitment to the project. It will also identify the project role and level of responsibility for each contributor, that is, lead curator, assistant curator and so on, and timescale for actions to be completed. The document should be approved by the board of management and the relationship between the board of management strategic document and this implementation document should be clear.

Client design brief

The client design brief is the first stage at which the internal client organisation project team contributes formally to the project process. It will develop from the client project brief prepared by the project director, and a key issue to be addressed is identification of the optimum extent of information that is to be included within it.

The client design brief has an obvious key role in the briefing process (see Figure 3.3). It synthesises the strategic and operational organisational issues with the project-specific issues from the client organisation's perspective and it is the first point at which the project aspirations are discussed with personnel outside the client organisation. In

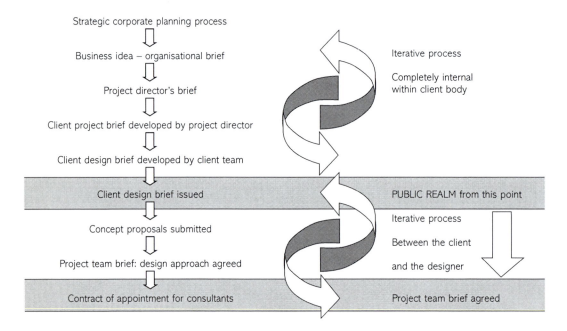

Figure 3.3   Developing the client design brief

addition to articulating the issues within the organisational brief noted earlier, it must also provide designers with key project and other technical information relating to the execution of the project in the context of addressing the needs of the operational business. It also has a vital purpose as an 'invitation to tender' and as such will become part of the formal contractual agreement between the client and the designer.

Given this multitude of purposes, a key issue for the client to manage is the provision of information for the design brief. This must set out the main project parameters without ambiguity while encouraging maximum creative input from the designer. While the danger of leaving out key information from the client design brief is clear, what is not so obvious is that providing too much information in an inflexible manner is equally damaging, through closing down business opportunities or conceptual approaches too early in the design process. Damaging also is too much information given in a vague manner.

For example, where a concept interpretative plan/report has been developed for a museum gallery it is enough to list main theme titles and sub-theme titles as text, with supplementary text information regarding priorities and the relationship between themes and or adjacent gallery spaces. At most, key theme titles may be diagrammatically placed as words on a plan of the intended gallery space. Information thus presented appears clear yet still fluid, permitting confident reinterpretation by each design practice. Intellectual interrelationships and priorities should be illustrated, not physical solutions.

Although it must clearly articulate specific project outcomes, the client design brief must avoid steering the design consultants towards any preconceived notions of preferred or 'intended conceptual design approach' if a truly unique solution is intended. To build in any preconceived outcomes at this stage will have the effect of neutralising the creative potential from the outset. Providing the optimum degree of information for a designer is only possible if the working methods of the designer are understood; hence the early parts of this book regarding the aims of a design practice. A client employs a designer to provide particular creative skills, breadth of design knowledge, and awareness of both historic and contemporary design issues and approaches, in addition to technical design skills that enable the design transformation process. It is therefore essential that the designer is permitted to exercise these skills fully as far as the project and its allocated resources permit. This will mean permitting the design consultant initially to push and test the conceptual design limits first thought appropriate by the client. Later chapters discuss how to assess objectively and utilise ambitious design concepts during the interview process.

The importance of the briefing process and the various stages of briefing development have now been outlined in some detail. The objective of the client design brief is to provide information to a range of shortlisted design practices in a manner that permits each to prepare a conceptual design approach. Each design concept should fulfil the business objectives. The range of concepts provides a variety of design approaches that will each impart differing benefits/opportunities to the client. The client design brief is also an invitation to tender that permits the preparation of a fee for each of the design approaches to be taken. However, even where a single design practice is being approached or a project is being undertaken by an in-house team, a client design brief is essential if a mutually satisfactory design process and design solution is to be achieved.

The following is suggested as a format for the information to be contained within the client design brief. Much like a design brief itself, it should serve as an outline template to stimulate preparation of a project-/client-specific brief. The headings are followed by further discussion of each point. Since such a document will contain input from many contributors, it is important that a single author is appointed to collate and edit the final document. This should be submitted to a client organisation's board of management for their approval before issue.

Client Design Brief

Section 1	Introduction	The project
		This document
		Timescale for presentation
		Budget
		Special operational/policy issues
		Contract terms
		Client contacts

Section 2	The Project Brief	
	Client Organisation	Core business
		Background to project
		Existing client team structure
	The Project	Existing situation
		Main objectives/scope of work
		Design criteria
		Consultant's role/relationship to other consultants
		Priorities
		Outline plans/sketches
	Client Timetable	Project completion and key dates
		Phasing
		Interview and consultant's appointments
	Budget Information	Approved level of expenditure
		Source of funds: funder's requirements
		Financial reporting requirements
		Approval requirements

Section 3	Interview/Presentation Requirements	Design information/presentation materials
		Report
		Overview of design philosophy
		Methodology

Project management
Programme
Cost report
Fee proposal
Practice information
Quality
Personnel
Health and safety
Insurance
References
Financial profile

Section 4   Instructions to Tenderers

Instructions to tenderers
Form of agreement
Supplementary information
Proposal return envelopes
Useful addresses
Assessment panel and criteria

Appendix

Survey information
   Site
   Building
   Existing structural assessment
   Existing services infrastructure
Photographs of site
Data sheets
Sales levels
Market share

Below is a detailed description of what each section should include.

Section 1   Introduction

The purpose of Section 1, 'Introduction', is to provide a summary of the project parameters to allow each invited design practice to review briefly all the key parameters of the project and of the concept preparation stage to assess whether or not they are in a position to respond to the design brief. To achieve this, the Introduction should be contained within two pages. The sub-headings should be written by the client project team along the following lines:

The project
Provide a brief outline of the project and 'scope of the works' in two or three short paragraphs, four at most. For example: 'Client organisation is inviting shortlisted

design consultants to prepare conceptual design approaches for the development of the area known as [the new retail identity]/ for a new theatre/ for a new night-club/ for a new gallery and so on with the intention of appointing a successful design practice as the lead consultant on the project.'

This document

Define the purpose of the design brief/invitation to tender document in one or two paragraphs, three at most. Note briefly the terms on which proposals at this stage are being sought, that is, flat fee, expenses only and so on. For example: 'This document forms a design brief/invitation to tender which has been issued to three shortlisted design practices to permit the preparation of conceptual design proposals for presentation to [client organisation]. These presentations will be made on [date] at [place] with an appointment being made to the successful consultant immediately thereafter. Presentation requirements are specified later in this document.

'A fixed fee of £xxx Exc. VAT will be payable to the unsuccessful consultants for completion of these design concept proposals to cover expenses. One selected design practice/design team will be appointed to take the project forward on the basis of their design and fee proposal.'

Timescale for presentation

Define the critical business timescale dates in a single paragraph, two at most. If appropriate, note key phases of the project relating to trading or other critical purposes. The client should also state that any design practice that submits a design concept proposal at a presentation stage must only do so if they have the resources necessary to complete all aspects of the project within this critical timeframe. If there will be financial or other business losses if the completion date is missed, the nature and extent of that loss should be stated here.

Budget

Give an overview of the budget and other financial parameters in one or two paragraphs. The client will ideally be in a position to state explicitly the maximum sum allocated to the project. If the design brief being issued is for a part of a larger project, the client should specify the sum on which design fees should be based. The client should also note that the design practice will be expected to provide details of their financial reporting methods in their presentation proposal, all as specified in more detail later in the design brief. Where funding is being provided by a third party this should be stated. Where such a funder has specific requirements it should be noted that further detail is given later in the brief.

Special operational/policy issues

The client organisation must clarify any operational and/or policy issues that the design consultant is obliged to incorporate into the design concept proposal. It must also clarify policy issues by which the design consultant must abide by agreeing to prepare a concept proposal. Although this will be covered in more detail in the form of appointment, stating important issues here as a core requirement of the appointment permits the design practice to evaluate their response to these conditions before carrying out any work. Policy issues may include copyright, confidentiality, energy management, disability access, financial reporting, funding body requirements and so on. Typically clients will wish to safeguard any sensitive market or financial information that would be of value to competitors, and may wish to control how the successful design consultant/team uses any information relating to the project for promotional purposes.

Contract terms

The client should refer to the *form of appointment* and *conditions of engagement* that will apply to the successful consultant. A single paragraph should suffice. If it is not included in the document, offer to send the consultants a copy of the form of appointment. This is also the place to state, if appropriate, that before appointment the successful consultant must submit three references and three years' accounts to the client contact. This is also the place to note, where appropriate, that all materials produced during the concept proposal stages will be returned to the designers, with the exception of the winning submission. This is the place to note that late submissions will not be accepted.

Client contacts

The client organisation should provide a single point of contact for all queries or requests for any further information referred to in the design brief, that is, technical queries on the brief, or invitation to tender, standard form of appointment, conditions of engagement and so on. Name, direct dial phone, e-mail address and the like should be given. On more complex projects a number of client contacts, each with a particular perspective, may be listed (design, finance, contracts, and so on). The position of the client contact relative to the project should be made clear. The client should offer the designers an opportunity to visit the site, and the procedures that the designer must follow in order to do so should be stated.

Section 2   The project brief

Client organisation

The purpose of this first section is to impart the overall character of the client organisation commissioning the project and give a sense of its values, its structure and its customer or client base. The client design brief should give a single-page overview of the client organisation. This clarifies the business context within which the design practice may place the design project. The information may comprise a brief history of the formation and development of the organisation, with some recent background pertaining to events leading to the need for the project. Some form of photographic images may assist. Finally, information relating to the existing project team structure and its relationship with the client organisation's ongoing business structure will be helpful.

The project

Providing clearly structured, hierarchically organised information for this section of the client design brief is one of the most difficult tasks of all. The nature and extent of the information that will be contained in this section will depend on the nature of the project, the nature of the client organisation and the personnel compiling the information.

The following lists set out generic information headings that should have appropriate detail supplied by the client project team. Project resources are considered as major sub-headings. This sub-heading is the core concept design information. It is important to set out all the information in a concise and logical hierarchical manner.

The existing situation

- Location of the project site
- Present use of project site (if applicable)
- Overall area in square metres. This should be cross-referred to the relevant drawing information
- Description and condition of the project site. Ground conditions if a green-field site, or condition of buildings or interior space as relevant
- Statistics relating to the area of the project (population, footprint area, collections and so on)
- Legal constraints: planning status, Crown exemption or title/other constraints. The client should give guidance on how to deal with these aspects at the concept design stage. The client should give a brief outline of the status of the site in relation to the local plan. It should be noted if the building is listed or if the site has particular archaeological significance.

Main objectives/scope of work

- The business case
- Scope of work (in general terms).

Design criteria

- General overview
- Intellectual design criteria
- Functional design criteria
- Technical design criteria
- Accommodation design criteria/detailed requirements to be incorporated
- Priorities.

Within the context of the overall project objectives, the detailed requirements of the design brief should now be set out. Where the project is of a large and complex nature a summarised design brief supplemented by further detail in an appendix is a good option. In the absence of a specific project requirement it is difficult to give details but Table 3.1 (on page 45) sets out some generic headings.

Table 3.1   Project – schedule of accommodation

Facility	Activities	Area, m²	Comments
Foyer	Description of activities	x	Comments
Reception	Description of activities	x	Comments
Shop	Description of activities	x	Comments
Café	Description of activities	x	Comments
Offices	Description of activities	x	Comments
Laboratories	Description of activities	x	Comments
Caretaker	Description of activities	x	Comments
Residential	Description of activities	x	Comments
Kitchen	Description of activities	x	Comments
External courtyard	Description of activities	x	Comments

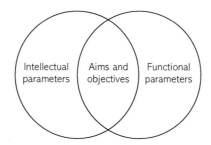

Figure 3.4   Main areas of concern

Although it does not have to be explicitly identified as such in a written design brief, the project design brief information falls into three main areas of concern: 'Aims and objectives', 'Intellectual parameters' and 'Functional parameters' (Figure 3.4). Whereas the functional parameters are objective and measurable, the intellectual parameters are subjective and are a matter of judgement. The means of achieving the aims and objectives will be informed by the mix of intellectual and functional parameters put in place by a client and this mix will be underpinned by the organisational culture of the client organisation (Figure 3.5).

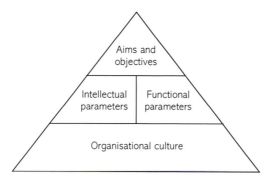

Figure 3.5   Organisational culture as foundation for project objectives

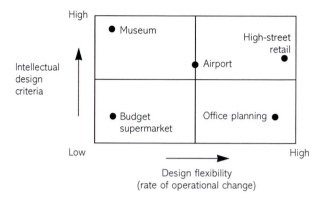

Figure 3.6   Intellectual design criteria and design flexibility as determinants

The extent of articulation of the conceptual design framework information required in a brief depends on the nature and complexity of the project. A speculative office building on a technology park site has an entirely different conceptual design framework from say a building society seeking a new identity for its national chain of high-street outlets linked to a revised marketing plan/identity. The intellectual framework will relate to many factors, some of which are listed below. Figure 3.6 considers the importance of intellectual design criteria relative to design flexibility – in itself related to the likely rate of change required.

The conceptual framework may include guidance on existing design principles established for the existing physical context of a site or building, and may also include marketing links, innovative standards, flexibility of design, quality standards, academic criteria and standards, sustainability criteria, energy efficiency criteria, physical and intellectual access, green issues such as recycling criteria and so on.

The functional aspects of the design brief will all be measurable and will include performance criteria such as key schedules of accommodation and other facilities required, with priorities stated, as in Table 3.1 on page 45.

Consultant's role on project/Consultant's relationship with other consultants
The brief must confirm the role that the design practice is expected to fulfil on the project, that is, acting as the lead consultant or as a sub-consultant with specific limited responsibilities. The relationship with any other project consultants who may already be appointed must be made clear.

Outline plan information
Suitable outline survey plan or diagrammatic sketch plan information should be provided.

Client timetable
The timetable for the project should be set out in narrative form and in a Gantt chart where possible. Key milestones relating to the project and the parallel organisational

business processes should be highlighted and given explanation where required. Holiday periods, financial reporting dates or the date of arrival of new equipment and/or staff are examples. The programme dates for the interview and appointment process should also be given.

Budget information

Budget information should be set out in narrative form, with supplementary tabular information as appropriate to the scale and complexity of the project. Some key figures that should be given are the total level of approved expenditure and the level of expenditure that should be used to calculate fees. Information relating to financial year accounting and or cash flow criteria should be specified. Where appropriate, information relating to the source of funds and any funders' requirements should be stated. Financial reporting requirements should be specified. Information relating to contingency sums and the management of contingencies should be made clear. Financial information should be set out excluding VAT.

Section 3   Interview/presentation requirements

The purpose of this section of the design brief is to 'give a shape to the response' desired from the design consultants. This phrase is used in preference to 'specify the response' for a particular reason. It is assumed that in seeking out a range of creative approaches to a design project the client is writing the design brief to seek proposals from a small number of design consultants each of whom is already assessed as capable of providing an appropriate professional design solution. The shortlisting selection criteria and process are dealt with in the next chapter. The presentation requirements section of the client design brief must therefore fulfil the client's wish to obtain design concept proposals which permit evaluation of the business criteria without limiting the scope for creative potential to be explored by each of the design consultants. The driving concern of course is to ensure that both issues are easy to understand and that it is possible to evaluate one set of design concept proposals against another. The difficulty for the client is to provide information which on the one hand seeks to be explicit regarding business objectives yet on the other must leave an optimum degree of freedom for each of the design consultants to pursue their own (unique) approach to fulfilling the objectives. For example, where a client organisation require new office space incorporating a reception/public space that reflects their involvement as a leading player in the computer games software market the brief should reflect this using adjectival descriptions, 'fun/sophisticated/high technology/accessible' and so on, rather than stating literal views on how the image might be achieved. If there is no scope to pursue differing creative approaches, then there is little point in approaching a number of design practices. There is a fine line for the client between giving clear yet specific information that permits interpretation, and giving information that is so specific as to predetermine the outcome. Part of this distinction rests within the level of detail expected by the client at this first stage.

As for any form of agreement between cooperative interested parties, it is essential to start the design development process by establishing mutually agreeable points of principle relating to overall approach before expecting agreement on points of detail. This section might therefore usefully start with a brief preamble that makes it clear that 'The client expects presentation materials that impart the general qualities and relationships of the conceptual design approach. As a guide to the extent of detail to be contained in the above, the client confirms that it is the overall conceptual approach which is being evaluated. Detailed proposals are not expected until further information is released and discussion is under way.'

Depending on the nature of the design project, this may be further supported by something like, 'The general spatial approach, specification of materials and finishes felt to be appropriate, in addition to the relationships of furniture/architecture/lighting/graphics/multimedia/space planning . . . should be made clear.'

It is also wise for a client to consider exactly how the presentation process will take place when determining what the presentation materials might comprise. At the very least there will be a formal presentation backed up with verbal support from the designers in attendance. This will require a very different set of presentation materials from the second-stage client analysis process, when the designers have left. This suggests that the designers must be encouraged to provide two levels of presentation materials – one to support their verbal presentation and a bound report that in their absence will reconstruct the design philosophy and provide further layers of analysis and comparison.

The response from each of the design practices will comprise not only 'soft' subjective design information relating to conceptual aesthetics and spatial organisation responses to the client brief, but will also contain 'hard' design information regarding contract management, contract administration, resourcing, budget and cost planning, critical path programming, fee structure and so on. It is therefore vital, notwithstanding the earlier concerns about not predetermining the outcome with overly specific briefing, that a format be set out to assist in evaluating responses fairly and to ensure that all key aspects of client briefing have been addressed. A general minimum level of information is suggested below.

Design information/presentation materials

Design information is the 'soft' subjective information that will be used to support a verbal presentation. The client should give a synopsis of what is expected as a *minimum* from the design practice in terms of drawings, plans, sections, key areas/treatments, models, story-boards, material boards and so on. Don't be too dogmatic as the nature and balance of presentation information will probably depend on the nature of the design approach. Some practices will favour drawings which, although conceptual, are also relatively specific, while others will provide conceptual sketches with models of various detailed aspects. The materials will impart not only the nature of the concept design approach but also the nature of the work of the practice. The key point is that the information should communicate the conceptual intent. If it doesn't communicate, don't assume that the problem is a lack of understanding on the part of the client. It may be a shortcoming of the design information. In some instances it may be wise to limit the amount of material to be contained on four to six A2 size boards or two to three A1 boards and so on, depending on the nature of the project and the amount of space available for the presentations.

Report

The report is required during the presentation for discussion, and post presentation to support individual design approaches without the designers being present. This comprises, although not exclusively, the 'hard' objective design information referred to earlier. Copies should be requested for all client parties who will take part in the selection process. The following are the section headings for the report that the client should use as a guide.

Overview of design philosophy

The report must start by stating the designer's philosophy underpinning their conceptual approach. The client should state that the design practice must keep this information to a single page. The designers may if they wish use a combination of text and images as this page should encapsulate their entire approach to the design.

Methodology

How do the design practice envisage that the concept finalisation, design development and production stages will take place? Where is the input of other consultants envisaged to complete the design team – that is, structural engineers, quantity surveyors, multimedia designers? How will these other consultants be engaged? Directly by the client or as a sub-consultant of the designer? How do they envisage preparing cost reports, detailed programming of ongoing activity? This heading should address aspects of the process such as consultation and approval processes, and is also an opportunity for the design practice to 'flag up' any areas of risk, including articulation of any implications arising from missing deadlines for critical client information and so on. If appropriate, the proposed project phasing strategy should be identified.

The personnel and other consultant resources that will be required to support the methodology should be stated. This is an important aspect as it permits the fee to be objectively tied to specific resources from specific personnel, an aspect that will become part of the contractual agreement. (See also 'Fee proposal' and 'Personnel'.)

Project management

The design practice should be asked to outline their project management experience and the project management methodology for the project. This should bear in mind any existing project management structure of the client project team and/or other consultant team already on board, as stated within the client design brief.

Programme

The design practice should prepare their own outline or critical path programme indicating key aspects of the overall project. As a minimum this should identify items such as design development stages, tender stages, reporting and approval stages, off-site production and on-site production stages. It should identify critical dates by which the client must supply key approvals and key items of information to achieve the programme.

Cost report

The design practice must prepare an outline budget breakdown indicating how the client's approved budget for the project will be allocated to the elements within their design concept. This information is vital for controlling aspirations during the design development stages. The design practice's methodology for providing the client with regular reports on costs during the construction and fabrication process should be specified. This should respond to the financial reporting requirements given within the client design brief, and should ideally have been prepared by the design consultant's intended design team quantity surveyor.

Fee proposal

The design practice must give full details of its proposed fee for the project. Expenses and exclusions must be clearly specified, along with any assumptions made. Where the design consultant is bringing other consultants on board, either as part of his own team or suggesting that the client employs the additional consultants direct, the scope of their work and the associated fee should also be specified. Where specific types of attendance are required by the client, for example long periods of on-site attendance, this should be identified. Payment stages related to work stages should be clear, and should correlate to the specific personnel, programme and RIBA plan of work stages.

Practice information

The design practice should be asked to list their experience of projects that are related to the nature of the client's project.

Quality

The design practice should be asked to state their approach and methodology for ensuring quality control of the design project process, including experience of, or holding of, current quality system qualifications.

Personnel

The design practice should have specified the personnel who will be involved in the project earlier in the methodology statement and should also have specified what their respective roles will be. A personal CV for each member of staff is essential. It will also be useful to have background information relating to the entire practice, staff numbers and so on. This may give an indication as to the relative value of design consultants' resourcing to be provided at various stages of the project.

Health and safety

The design practice should state qualifications and management systems relating to health and safety. In particular, experience and knowledge of the Construction Design and Management Regulations should be provided. Any qualifications should be listed and evidence provided.

Insurance

The design practice should be asked to confirm the current level of Professional Indemnity insurance held and to supply evidence. Other insurances should also be confirmed where specifically requested by a client organisation.

References

The design practice should be asked to provide three references. The client should state within the design brief that all references will be taken up, and that an appointment is conditional on satisfactory responses from all referees. It is wise to follow this procedure through. A related question is whether the practice has at present, or has had in the past, any disputes with previous clients.

Financial profile

Where appropriate, the last three years' financial accounts of each practice may be requested for analysis. It should be noted that this information will be treated with confidence.

Section 4   Instructions to tenderers

The instructions to tenderers section should list all the requirements to be included within the tender return and should identify how many copies must be returned, to whom they should be returned, what they should be returned in, and the time and date by which they should be returned. These are all important aspects to pre-specify to ensure ease of management on tender return day.

The assessment procedure, including the panel of assessors to be present and the criteria to be used for assessing, should be specified. Where relevant, reference may be made to *Selecting Consultants for the Team: Balancing Quality and Price*, produced by the Construction Industry Board.[1]

- List of requirements
    (See Section 3, Interview/presentation requirements)
- Date and time for return of tenders
- Contact/address for return of tenders. Note if a special envelope has been supplied, this must be used for anonymous returns
- Supplementary information
    - Certificate of Bona fide/non-collusion tender return
    - Form of Agreement
    - EC Procurement Directives or other UK legislation (for example local authority 'Best Value')
    - Useful addresses
- Assessment panel and criteria

- Presentation requirements: overhead projector, projector/projector screen, flipchart board, table for models and so on.

Appendix

Information to be contained in appendices or a supplementary document should include any technical background data relating to the site of the project and any relevant client organisation business data. This may include survey information, dimensional data, structure and services in drawn or photographic form and the like, and data sheets of accommodation requirements/relationships, plant or other operational information.

- Mechanical and electrical services information (if applicable)
- Services: public utilities to site or within site if known. Water supply and sewage, electricity, gas, telephone and so on.

The client should conclude by noting that while the above is believed to be accurate, the successful design practice must prepare its own survey and verification of all statutory approvals for detail design stages. Location plans of the existing site proposed for the project should be cross-referred to the relevant drawing information.

Project team design brief

The project team brief will be completed only upon selection of a design team – the topic for the next chapter of this book. The distinction between the project team design brief and the client design brief is very important, although literal differences between the two are likely to be small. The project team design brief is 95–98 per cent identical to the client design brief, but with the concept design approach and methodology developed by the successful design team built in. As such it is a document which now 'belongs to everyone' and will serve to unify all project contributors from this point forward. In many cases the project team design brief will not become a 'bound' and completed document, with the changes to the client design brief perhaps only recorded on the design team concept drawings or perhaps minuted as part of a report recommending the appointment of the successful design team. Often at this stage of a project the pace changes dramatically, with all contributors focused on achieving progress. Ideally, however, a separate document incorporating the client design brief with the concept will be produced and incorporated into the design team contractual agreement.

NOTE

1. Construction Industry Board, *Selecting Consultants for the Team: Balancing Quality and Price*, 2nd edn, London: Thomas Telford Publishing, 2000.

4 Shortlisting design consultants

PURPOSE

The purpose of this chapter is to set out an objective methodology for identifying and shortlisting design practices. It examines this process and follows through to the point of achieving a shortlist of design practices which have been assessed by the client organisation project team as the most appropriate consultants to receive a client design brief/invitation to tender. The chapter starts with a brief consideration of the types of design practice that may be required for a design project.

It is assumed that client organisations have control over their own selection and evaluation processes. However, reference is also made to EC procurement directives and UK/other legislation which may affect public-sector client organisations in particular.

OUTLINE

- Introduction
- The external project team
- Completing the design team
- Identifying all possible designers/consultants
- Setting client criteria for shortlisting designers and other consultants
- First approaches
- Preparing a shortlist
- Shortlist report to board of management
- Completion of shortlisting – selection of a successful practice.

The following related matters are also discussed at the end of the chapter:

- Notifying unsuccessful consultants
- Maintaining a database of consultants
- Internal versus external design team.

INTRODUCTION

The process outlined in this chapter for shortlisting design practices may equally be applied to shortlisting other project consultants. Often the lead consultant will wish to put forward names of other professional consultants required to support and complete the project team and to advise on the level of other consultants' fees for the input involved. The lead consultant must be fully supported by sympathetic professional consultant 'partners' in addition to the client project team during the project.

Where a project is large and/or complex and the client has already fully acknowledged that a range of consultants or a 'consortium' approach will be required, the process will remain the same. In the consortium context, the design practice being identified for potential shortlisting will be judged on their ability not only to design but also to act as lead consultant, involving design management skills.

The approach outlined in this chapter is obviously not the only basis on which to proceed, but it does provide a model that may be adapted to suit particular requirements. It assumes that clients will make their final selection of a design consultant based on the evaluation of a number of alternative outline concept proposals prepared by shortlisted design consultants following a briefing meeting, before a final appointment is made. It avoids the all-too-common situation where designers are shortlisted and issued with a brief and immediately asked to attend a presentation/interview where an outline proposal, prepared in isolation and without any dialogue with the client, is expected to be presented and evaluated. Such an approach misses out many layers of opportunity for client and designer alike, and may even create distance through a lack of communication, information exchange, exploration of design direction and potential for teamworking synergy.

The steps in the recommended procedure are as follows:

- Client organisation to identify suitable consultants
- Client organisation to issue letter of inquiry/request for practice brochures
- Initial client selection process based on brochures/previous experience
- Formal approval of shortlist by client organisation board of management
- Issue of client design brief to shortlisted consultants
- Informal briefing meeting
- Formal presentation/interview
- Formal evaluation of design concept and fee proposals
- Appointment of successful design practice.

The shortlisting process outlined here is one that initially involves no input from personnel outside the client body other than the submission of practice brochures. All initial shortlisting activity involves the client selecting suitable candidates from word of mouth, existing marketing and promotional material and/or the client's knowledge of recent related work.

The process of issuing a brief to the shortlisted design consultants and the evaluation of the responses is covered in the next chapter of this book. It is worth stating at this point, however, that no speculative or free work is expected or requested from any consultants at any point within this framework.

THE EXTERNAL PROJECT TEAM

The term 'external project team' refers to those members of the wider project team who are not directly employed by the client organisation. Few clients, if any, directly employ the full range of in-house personnel for all stages of a project.

External personnel for the project must first of all be identified as suitable for the project; that is, they must either have suitable direct experience or transferable experience for the project type which the client has in mind. Assuming that the project is buildings or interior design related – three-dimensional and multidisciplinary in nature – the external design team is likely to comprise a wide range of professional disciplines in addition to architects and designers. Many disciplines will be unfamiliar to many clients unless the organisation has an estates department or is involved in ongoing series of capital expenditure projects as part of its core operation. For example a university estates department is continually involved in the refurbishment and redesign of all types of property from research laboratories, lecture theatres/classrooms, staff office areas, student leisure facilities in addition to developing new student residencies equipped to ever increasing standards and holiday letting during summer months and so on. However, not all organisations have this type of in-house resource.

For information, a list of potential external project team contributors is given below. The list is divided into pre-project, project and post-project stages, although the boundaries will sometimes overlap. The stages of each process will generally remain clearly identifiable even where overlap occurs.

This list is not exhaustive but is intended as a guide. The number of differing external project team contributors required on any part of a project will depend on the nature and complexity of the project and/or client organisation.

Pre-project (evaluation)

- Management consultants
- Economic appraisal consultants
- Marketing consultants
- Public relations consultants
- Lead and specialist consultants
  - Architects, designers
  - Town planners
  - Environmental consultants
- Local authorities – planning, building control, roads, water, drainage
- Public utilities – electricity, gas, telecoms
- Enterprise agencies
- Government agencies – SEPA, Health and Safety Executive, FE, and so on
- Funding bodies – Lottery Fund distributors (various) and so on.

Project

- Lead designers (assumes 3D multidisciplinary project)
  – Architects
  – Interior designers
  – Exhibition designers
  – Industrial designers
  – Product designers
- Specialist designers
  – Structural and civil engineers
  – Mechanical and electrical consulting engineers
  – Graphic designers
  – Web designers
  – Multimedia designers
  – Landscape designers
  – Acoustics designers
  – Lighting designers
  – Artists (public art or commissioned pieces)
- Quantity surveyors
- Structural engineers
- Civil engineers
- Town planning consultants
- Interpreters
- Project managers
- Contractors
  – Main contractors
  – Specialist subcontractors
- Planning supervisors.

Post-project

- Facilities managers
- Maintenance contractors
- Public relations consultants
- Photographers
- Publishers
- The press and the media.

COMPLETING THE DESIGN TEAM

It is useful to note in general terms what type of services key consultants will bring to a project. The intention of this brief narrative is not to list exhaustively all the services provided in a contractual sense but rather to give a sense of the general contribution and the professional relationships of each with other project team members. For a listing of standard services at various stages of a project, the advisory organisations listed in Chapter 6 should be approached. Services provided by any professional will relate to the contractual agreement entered into with the client.

Design manager

Reporting to the project director, the design manager has the task of leading and coordinating all inputs to the design project, whether from within or outside the client organisation. A key task is communication of information and intent, to ensure that the client project team and the external project team are fully aligned and able to function effectively, and that the client organisation's board of management are fully informed. Often the role involves a high degree of coordination of inputs from within the client organisation. The design management role is a more proactive role than a normal project management role. Exact services will vary from project to project and client to client.

Designer/architect

On straightforward projects the designer/architect leads the input of the other design team consultants. In addition to providing a client organisation with conceptual designs and direction, the lead designer/architect develops the concept design into a completed set of working drawings and written specifications, simultaneously coordinating the other design inputs from structural engineers, mechanical and electrical engineers, lighting designers, graphic designers and other consultants as an intrinsic part of the design process.

The designer/architect also leads the design team during the tender stages when the design team working drawings/specifications and other contract documents prepared by the quantity surveyor are issued to selected contractors to permit competitive costs to be obtained.

During the construction phase the designer/architect will continue to act as the lead consultant, coordinating the input of other consultants. The lead consultant has traditionally also acted as contract administrator, a role which is described later in the book.

Quantity surveyor

The early appointment of a quantity surveyor is advisable. The quantity surveyor provides cost-reporting information at all stages of a project from early cost planning at conceptual evaluation stages through to monthly cost reports and cash flow during contract work stages. The quantity surveyor can also provide a strong source of contractual advice generally beyond that of the designer/architect.

Structural engineer

The structural engineer provides design input usually relating only to the structural design aspects of a project. On the majority of projects the structural engineer will have no proactive input to aesthetics other than as the outcome of structural calculations and specifications. Since structural solutions can have a major impact on aesthetics, the designer/architect will usually give guidance to the structural engineer as to the nature of appropriate visual solutions together with a client's performance specification, to which the engineer will apply calculations and a final specification for the approval of the designer/architect.

Mechanical and electrical consulting engineers

The consultant mechanical and electrical engineers provide design input on the air handling, heating and electrical services design respectively. Since air handling ductwork and electrical services trunking and outlets can be large physically and can therefore have a major impact on aesthetics, the designer/architect will usually give guidance as to the nature of appropriate visual solutions or physical organisational constraints and an appropriate performance specification for implementation by the engineer.

IDENTIFYING ALL POSSIBLE DESIGNERS/CONSULTANTS

The selection of designers and other consultants provides the first test of the client's internal project team and the client organisation reporting and approval mechanisms. Many valuable lessons will be gained by the team and by the organisation during these stages, and any areas of concern or weakness regarding communication or conflicting roles/levels of authority in particular should be addressed.

Depending on the business sector of the client and their previous experience of project work, initially identifying suitable personnel will either prove to be an easy task or may leave a client wondering where and how to start.

Making contact with the appropriate professional body of each professional discipline will usually provide clients with a list of potential consultants (see page 174). It will also provide a source of standard 'form of appointment' contracts that clients will wish to tailor to their own specific project use. All the professionals will require individual form of appointment contracts, and a checklist of issues is given in Chapter 6 to assist with the preparation of the contracts, conditions of engagement and appendices required. Each contract should be customised to suit particular project and client organisation requirements, and to suit the law of the country in which the contract will apply.

From the initial point of discussion within a client organisation regarding the selection of suitable design consultants it is important that the client team that will take the project forward are involved in the process of identifying and shortlisting candidates to interview.

When initially drawing together names of consultants, it is wise to spread the net as widely as possible so that the subsequent narrowing-down processes may take place without nagging doubts that any suitable candidates may have been overlooked. The team should continually be given the confidence to look forward and not to feel the need to revisit old decisions.

Depending on the nature of the client organisation and the level of expenditure involved, other statutory selection procedures may be involved. In particular, public sector organisations are required to follow EC procurement directives and other UK legislation when inviting tenders for works of any description when values go above a threshold value. EC procurement directives exist to ensure that all suppliers in the EC's member states are treated equally. Key points as given by the Construction Industry Board are:

- The regulations apply to all contracts whose value exceeds specified thresholds.
- Notice of contracts for which tenders are sought must be published in the *Official Journal of European Communities*; minimum periods for replies at selection and tendering stages are specified in the regulations.
- Authorities must use objective, non-discriminatory criteria for specifying requirements, selecting those to be invited to tender and for awarding contracts. These criteria must be declared in the *OJEC* notice and in the invitation to tender respectively and no criteria other than the declared are permitted.
- Procedures are specified for debriefing unsuccessful candidates.[1]

While the above is accurate at the time of writing, further guidance is available on: www.hm-treasury.gov.uk

Local authority procedures also include 'best value' initiatives driven by legislation which changes at not infrequent intervals. Local authority and other 'defined authorities' controlled by such legislation must keep abreast of all requirements and practices that are current at the time of project planning.

The risk of a client organisation making multiple enquiries to consultants should be avoided, as this will give the impression of a client with poorly coordinated internal communication systems. Any basic signal of uncertainty from a client at this early stage will undermine many other well-considered and well-planned communications. An internal methodology should therefore be agreed for coordinating and collating the enquiries issued. One member of staff, usually the project director, should set a timescale for achieving a list of agreed enquiry contacts, giving guidelines to allocated team members.

In addition to word-of-mouth contacts, knowledge of projects carried out for competitors or by other organisations, contact with the professional bodies mentioned earlier and listed at the end of the book or scanning current design/trade journals provides several immediate sources of potential contacts, whatever the strategy. Where appropriate or required by legislation, the project may have to be advertised to attract information/enquiries from appropriate consultants.

SETTING CLIENT CRITERIA FOR SHORTLISTING DESIGNERS AND OTHER CONSULTANTS

When a number of client personnel are given the task of identifying potentially suitable design consultants it is essential that the criteria that the organisation wishes to use for selecting the shortlisted consultants at this stage are made clear. This will permit controlled and objective progress to be made by all contributors. At this stage a key selection criterion that must be objectively specified is the degree to which the client organisation is prepared to engage with the design process as an exploratory iterative process, as opposed to a technical enabling process.

The criteria may range simplistically from making a *safe* selection using known and proven design criteria – say by limiting the selection to design practices that have recently completed comparable projects or previous work for the organisation – to the other end of the creative and risk strategy spectrum by determining that an innovative and cutting-edge solution is expected or aspired to. The market sector of the client organisation, their strategy for achieving competitive advantage and the level of strategic significance of the project to the organisation will all govern this decision.

For clients in a cost-led market sector or clients who are following a cost-led business strategy, an innovative design strategy is unlikely to deliver a match of expectations to aspirations. A safe design strategy is most appropriate where design acts as a facilitator or technical enabler and where intellectual/conceptual design input is at a minimum. However, an innovative design strategy will be essential for clients who gain competitive advantage through a differentiation strategy.

An important factor for clients from any market sector, following any business strategy, to be aware of is that as innovative design increases, so too does the potential level of exposure to financial risk and risk to programme. Risk is inherent in any innovative context, although appropriate management can reduce that risk.

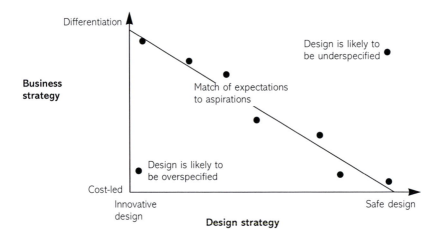

Figure 4.1   Relationship of design strategy to business strategy

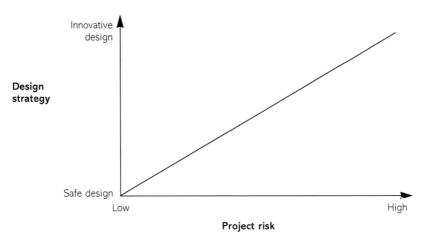

Figure 4.2   Relationship of project risk to design strategy

These two generic extremes of design approach have characteristics that may be depicted as in Figures 4.1 and 4.2.

Figure 4.1 indicates that an appropriate relationship of design strategy to business strategy exists around the line of best fit. Above this line, as business strategy moves from a cost-led basis into a differentiation strategy, the design approach should be guided towards an innovative design strategy, optimised on the line. Similarly, below the line, as a business moves towards a cost-led business strategy, design should be guided towards a safe design approach, optimised on the line. Of course there is no formula for calculating a precise 'line of best fit'; however, the figure does illustrate the logical relationship.

The relationship of project risk to design strategy should be clearly understood by client organisations when embarking on a project. An innovative design strategy by its very nature inherently carries the risk of programme and finance difficulties, and indeed product or end use difficulties through exploration of previously 'uncharted waters'. Such risk and failure will be unsustainable for a cost-led business. The relationships are set out in order that client organisations may form appropriate aspirations to match design strategy with business strategy and to put an appropriate risk management strategy in place. For innovative design strategies this may mean acceptance of higher fee structures *and* a move from a pure business relationship towards a partnering arrangement with the design team if success is to be achieved. The design strategy selection is a key aspect for client organisations to be aware of and integrate into their design brief documentation and concept evaluation processes if a 'best fit' of aspirations to end result, and design process, is to be achieved.

Although these two levels of design approach/creativity are at opposite ends of the spectrum in terms of intellectual input and risk control, the criteria for assessing design proposals based on each approach are actually the same but must have an appropriately adjusted emphasis – does the design proposal satisfy the brief?

FIRST APPROACHES

Having identified consultants appropriate to the design strategy intended, a variety of first-approach methodologies to design practices is obviously possible and will depend on a number of factors:

- The scale of the project
- The complexity of the project
- The project resources available to the client
- External/legislative requirements
- The familiarity of any existing professional relationship.

For simple and/or small-scale projects a telephone call outlining the nature of the intended project in general terms, including reference to budget and timescale, and seeking a current practice brochure, will suffice in gathering initial data and establishing interest.

For larger-scale and more complex projects, although the same basic information is required a more formal and structured approach is advisable. A standard written invitation to designers to register interest in the project and put forward their credentials is recommended. Information relating to particular aspects of the project may be requested from the designer. This will provide a more consistent set of responses with scope for objective assessment.

The contents of an initial enquiry to consultants, whether an informal verbal or formal written approach is made, may be as follows:

- Introduce the client organisation
- Outline the nature of the project
  - Design intent
  - Budget
  - Project timescale
- Outline the next stages of the client shortlisting/selection/interview process, with an estimate of timescale
- Enquire if the design practice/consultant is interested in and has the necessary resources available for the project
- Request a practice brochure and staff CVs
- Request recent references.

Whether a written invitation or a phone call is made to request initial practice information, the information issued by the design practices should not only be circulated to all client organisation internal project personnel but also recorded and structured in a manner which permits collective discussion and evaluation. In addition to permitting an objective decision to be made within the client's organisation, this will also provide an audit trail of the decision-making and decision-taking process.

The selection process beyond this initial internal trawl becomes more complex and necessarily onerous, and guidelines are given for the process. A major difficulty is the evaluation of qualitative issues relative to the straightforward financial and other quantitative assessments.

PREPARING A SHORTLIST

On receipt of a range of design practice brochures the immediate task is circulation of the information to the client organisation project team for their comment and assessment regarding suitability for shortlisting. This is a task that should be coordinated by the project director or his appointed representative, and forms the basis on which a decision will be made to shortlist a practice.

The selection criteria for preparing a shortlist will be based in the main on those shown in Figure 4.3.

Until this stage there has been no attempt to assess the information gathered from the design consultants identified other than in the most general of terms. Collating the responses in this way enables a simple scoring procedure to be carried out. This permits all team members to contribute to the process and an objective team decision to be reached either at a team meeting or by individual response. Individual contributors may supply information to the project director or his representative, who should maintain a single spreadsheet coordinating input from the individual contributors thus ensuring a uniform application of scoring.

Where appropriate to the ongoing business needs of a client organisation, this scoring information will also prove useful in maintaining a client database. Developing more detailed answers to these points will be taken further during the concept proposal and interview stages.

SHORTLIST REPORT TO BOARD OF MANAGEMENT

A report on the outcome of the initial information-gathering, shortlisting process and shortlist conclusions should be prepared by the project director for consideration and approval by the client organisation's board of management. The project director should also organise a meeting to present the report.

It is worth remembering that in addition to seeking their formal approval, the project director is also approaching the client organisation's board of management at this stage to permit their continued involvement in the decision-making process. The report should be no longer than two to three pages of main text plus supporting

	Consultants (mark out of 10, where 0 is minimum, and 10 is maximum)							
	A	**B**	**C**	**D**	**E**	**F**	**G**	**H**
• Design ability Creativity Teamworking Other								
• Management skills Design Project/contract Financial Other								
• Resources Personnel Locality Other								
• Experience Specific Transferable Other								
• Cause for concern? • Other								
Total								

Figure 4.3   Selection criteria – score sheet

appendices or handouts, which may contain full brochures or key extracts of design consultants' brochures and so on. The report should be structured as follows:

- Executive summary
- Introduction to the project
- Purpose of the report and actions required
- Actions to date (methodology and basis of selection)
- Conclusions
- Recommendations
    - For shortlist of design consultants
    - For action:
        Interview process
        Issue of brief for preparation of design concepts
        Presentation of concepts
        Appointment of successful consultant
- Next meeting – agree criteria for assessing design concept proposals
- Appendices
    - Practice literature
    - Scoring sheet
    - Programme.

The purpose of the report is to update the board of management, and to include them in the decision-making process, thus ensuring that the project moves forward on a basis which is formally approved and underwritten by the client organisation and not simply driven by the views of individuals. An audit trail is automatically generated. Some key decisions and approvals required are:

- How many designers to shortlist? (three to four seems adequate; more will lead to difficulties)
- Who are the shortlisted designers to be? Why? – Project director's report to be discussed noting the recommendations given
- Approval of a fee for concept proposals and interview stage – for unsuccessful designers
- Timescale
- The criteria and process for assessing design concepts/fee proposals
- Future board of management involvement – that is, representative present at presentations? Or future reports only? – board of management decision.

At the report stage it may be wise to include one or two additional design practices where debate is required to determine the final shortlisted consultants, that is, six names where it is intended to shortlist four, and thus engage board of management pro-actively in the decision process. As an example, at one such presentation, the director of the client organisation recommended shortlisting a practice which had not until that point been included within the top four candidates. The practice then went on to produce the successful design for a prestigious gallery space, beating the other shortlisted design practices.

COMPLETION OF SHORTLISTING – SELECTION OF A SUCCESSFUL PRACTICE

After the shortlist has been approved by the board of management, the next stage is the formal issue of the client design brief as an invitation to prepare a tender/design concept to the three to six (maximum) shortlisted design practices. This is covered in more detail in the next chapter.

NOTIFYING UNSUCCESSFUL CONSULTANTS

Following the preparation of the final shortlist of designers it is good practice to inform the unsuccessful consultancies that they have not been selected for the shortlist. Where appropriate, they may also be told that their information will be retained and included on the client's database of consultants.

MAINTAINING A DATABASE OF CONSULTANTS

Where clients have an ongoing need to work with designers for projects, a centrally controlled and generally available database is a sensible internal management resource for future design projects, this encourages the organisation to learn from its experience.

INTERNAL VERSUS EXTERNAL DESIGN TEAM

For some client organisations a choice will have to be made between using internal and external personnel to resource a project. It will be important to arrive at an objective decision to ensure that morale is maintained within the organisation. To this end an

SWOT Analysis In-house Team

Strengths of the in-house team 1. 2. 3. 4.	**Weaknesses** of the in-house team 1. 2. 3. 4.		**Strengths** of external consultants 1. 2. 3. 4.	**Weaknesses** of external consultants 1. 2. 3. 4.
Opportunities of using the in-house team on the project 1. 2. 3. 4.	**Threats** of using the in-house team on the project 1. 2. 3. 4.	Compare	**Opportunities** of using external consultants on the project 1. 2. 3. 4.	**Threats** of using external consultants on the project 1. 2. 3. 4.

SWOT Analysis External Consultants

Figure 4.4   Framework for a SWOT analysis

explicit and objective methodology should be developed for carrying out a cost–benefit appraisal comparing the use of in-house professional resources with external consultants for the project in question. It will help to carry out a SWOT analysis (Strengths/Weaknesses/Opportunities/Threats) in relation to the in-house team and external consultants (Figure 4.4).

During the SWOT analysis the factors to be considered include:

- Characteristics of the in-house team – What is the nature of their normal workload? Is there excess capacity? Can additional staff be employed? Will other activities suffer if in-house staff are appointed to a project? For example, a local authority in-house design team is likely to be operating at or near to 'capacity' supporting a multitude of personnel and departments preparing or advising on interiors, exhibitions, publications, advertisements, internal communications, emergency public notices and so on, leaving little or no resources available for capital projects particularly ambitious time consuming ones. The consistent and flexible application of a corporate identity will be a major drain on in-house design resources and may be a major task which is little appreciated within some areas of its host organisation
- Economics – Is the project capital funded or revenue funded? Are there legislative or funders' requirements to be satisfied regarding tendering procedures?
- Strategic priorities – Are there conflicting project versus ongoing operation priorities to be resolved? Is there a potential staff or other conflict of interest?
- Resources – Are there conflicting project versus ongoing operation resourcing difficulties to be resolved?
- Project characteristics – What is the overriding requirement of the project – creativity or technical enabling?
- External business environment PEST analysis (Political/Environmental/Social/Technological).

Typically the main benefits of each group may be set out as in Figure 4.5.

In-house team	External consultants
Availability	Greater creative input
Familiarity	Variety of approach
Convenience	Choice
Economy	Business relationship

Figure 4.5   Benefits of in-house team and of external consultants

NOTE

1. Construction Industry Board, *Selecting Consultants for the Team: Balancing Quality and Price*, London: Thomas Telford Publishing, 2000.

5 Presentation of concepts and assessment of proposals

PURPOSE

The purpose of this chapter is to outline a methodology for issuing the client design brief/invitation to tender to the design practices shortlisted by the process described in the previous chapter. This chapter takes the process to the point of identifying the successful design practice through an objective interview process which incorporates evaluation of the design proposals prepared by the shortlisted design practices. The design of an appropriate 'form of appointment' contract for the successful consultant is discussed in Chapter 6.

OUTLINE

- Introduction
- Issue of client design brief/invitation to tender
- Initial informal briefing meeting
- The presentation and interview process
- The evaluation process
- Notifying unsuccessful consultants.

INTRODUCTION

One of the main emphases of this book is the importance of the role of the client in the design process and the impact that effective design management within a client organisation has on the qualitative aspects of design team relationships, at all stages of the project. In large part this relates to ensuring consistent briefing, the effective flow of client information and the stability provided through integrated client approval processes. The interview stage presents particular challenges.

At this stage, having agreed a shortlist of design practices, the client has in effect concluded that any of the practices shortlisted has the credentials, experience and the creative and technical abilities required to carry out the project. Even at this early stage each shortlisted practice should be treated as potential team members and not kept at arm's length from the client team. The purpose now is to ensure that the project and all contributors are given the maximum opportunity to understand the client's business criteria and to explore creative directions within the client design brief.

A fee should be paid to all shortlisted designers who prepare proposals but who are unsuccessful on this occasion. The level of fee may simply cover expenses or be more, and constitutes a gesture of inclusion at this stage. This gesture minimises the uncertainty felt by any business in undertaking speculative work. Obviously the scale of the project will determine whether this approach is practicable and the level of fee proposed. For clients with an ongoing programme of projects it also establishes a good working relationship with the design community generally.

The methodology is as follows:

- The client organisation issues the shortlisted designers with the client design brief, inviting them to prepare concept design proposals
- The client organisation arranges informal briefing meetings with the designers to visit the project location, discuss the project and the client body as an organisation
- The shortlisted designers prepare proposals 'off site'
- The client organisation hosts a formal presentation and interview process
- The client organisation evaluates the design proposals
- The client organisation selects the successful consultant
- The client organisation notifies the unsuccessful consultants.

ISSUE OF CLIENT DESIGN BRIEF/INVITATION TO TENDER

The various stages of the overall briefing process have already been outlined earlier in the book, and an outline of a client design brief was discussed in Chapter 3. The brief should be issued under formal cover of a letter from the project director or his representative, with clear instructions regarding the next stages of the project process. The covering letter should include:

- Main client contact or contacts: name, phone, email
- A list of the enclosures
- Dates by which the informal briefing session will be held
- Dates that formal presentation of designers' proposals will be made
- Confirmation of fee for this stage to unsuccessful design practices
- An indication of the number of design practices being approached at this stage
- Offer of a debriefing meeting for unsuccessful consultants.

INITIAL INFORMAL BRIEFING MEETING

Following the issue of the client design brief, an informal briefing meeting gives designers and clients the opportunity to gain a feel for the values and approach, and indeed the personalities, of the other. It also provides an opportunity for designers to view and photograph the site or location and to discuss the project with the client, raising queries and gaining clarity as well as making the subsequent formal presentation and interview process less daunting for all.

Given that the reason for approaching several shortlisted designers is to explore comprehensively the creative direction of a client design brief, it is obvious that this informal stage can play an important part in exploring the full potential the project offers in both business and in creative terms.

It will be of value to both parties if as much time as possible is given to the informal briefing discussion process. This meeting will provide much source material for reading between the lines of the brief and will be important to a designer in giving them information so that they can interpret the brief confidently and layer their own distinctive creative personality into the project.

Some client organisations may wish to carry out the informal briefing meeting with all shortlisted design consultants in attendance simultaneously. This certainly has the benefit of being seen to provide each tendering practice with equal levels of briefing information. A further approach is to issue the client design brief tender documentation at a pre-tender briefing meeting. Both of these approaches, however, may restrict the free exchange of one-to-one views. Where time and legislative procedures permit, the preferred route is that of individual meetings.

Queries from tendering design practices

Following the initial interview, formal written questions should be welcomed from each of the tendering consultants. Responses to all questions should be issued to all tendering consultants. The identity of the practices asking the questions need not be revealed.

Designers prepare proposals

Following on from the informal briefing session and before the presentation interview process, the designers will be preparing their concept design, fee and resourcing proposal off site. A period of around three weeks is suggested as the optimum, two weeks being too short and four weeks perhaps too long, in providing time for indecision. While the optimum duration obviously depends on the complexity of the project, the intention should be to provide a period during which the designer's energies may be focused to the maximum extent on the project at their own conceptual level.

Receipt of proposals/tenders

The design proposals/tenders may be received in a number of ways; the selected route must of course be specified in the instructions to tenderers in the client design brief. The report element of the design proposal (see Chapter 3), which includes drawn and

Tender register			
Client:			
Contract name:			
Date			
	Time opened	Consultant/contractor	Tender fee/sum
1			
2			
3			
4			
5			
6			

Tenders opened in the presence of   _____

and witnessed by   _____

Tenders sent for tender report to   _____

By   _____

Date   _____

Figure 5.1   Example of a tender register

written design information with associated fee and resourcing information, may be returned on its own for client assessment before an interview/presentation, or the report information may be tabled at the presentation. While selection of the most appropriate route will depend on the scale of the project/client organisation, it is suggested that the report aspect of the tenders is submitted before the presentation interview. Whatever the route for receiving the information, a tender register should be maintained, an example of which is given in Figure 5.1. Where tenders are opened before interview, the tender register should wherever possible be signed by two individuals from the client organisation.

THE PRESENTATION AND INTERVIEW PROCESS

Factors to be considered when arranging the presentations and interview process are discussed in what follows.

Venue

The venue should be large enough to accommodate all attendees and any presentation equipment and materials.

Although the presentation must be formal in terms of information-gathering and guided by a standard agenda to ensure consistency, given that the designers will come to the presentation with differing forms of design team, design proposal and presentation materials and so on, a feeling of design team dialogue rather than an 'us and them' division should be engendered. All the designers will be well aware that they are not yet part of the client project team, so there is little point in emphasising this fact at this stage. The maximum amount of information should be extracted from the presentation, the final part of the pre-appointment process.

It should be reasonably simple to establish a supportive venue and environment, by considering, for example, seating arrangements and facilities.

This book at all times emphasises fostering a feeling of a team approach, even at the stages where a final team has not yet been assembled. This includes the presentation and interview process. Distancing may be created unintentionally by many factors, and is evidence of a lack of care and consideration.

MKW, an exhibition design practice, recall being called to interview by a large client organisation and being informed that an informal interview would take place. Upon arrival, they were faced by perhaps a dozen client personnel seated around a large U-shaped table, from which their own seating arrangement was spaced some 4–5 metres or so, thus creating both a literal and a metaphorical distance. For good measure, the overhead projector requested had a badly scratched glass-top surface and the image was projected not on to a screen, but on to a stucco wall, rendering the image useless. The practice, which had spent considerable time preparing their proposal, felt wrong-footed from the moment they entered the presentation room.

McKinstrie Wilde Millhouse Design, a graphic design practice, recall being asked to present their proposals for a new graphic identity as part of their ongoing work for a large client organisation in a room with inadequate lighting. Discussions rapidly degenerated into disagreements over colour, an argument impossible to resolve without adequate daylighting.

Equipment

Each design consultant should be asked to state any particular requirements they may have in terms of equipment for the presentation – overhead projector, flipchart and so on – within the client design brief (see instructions to tenderers, Chapter 3). If models are expected as a part of the presentation, a table large enough to display and view them will be required. Adequate and convenient power or other services must be provided by the client organisation.

Roles of attendees

The presentation meeting should be chaired by the project director and each aspect of the client body should be represented. During the introduction process the role of each member of staff or client board of management in attendance should be briefly outlined to the design team. Similarly the roles of all attendees from the design consultants team should be clear: the overall design team leader, project manager, specialist areas of support, that is graphic design, audiovisual design and so on.

Structuring a day of multiple presentations

Organising, coordinating and attending/chairing a full day of presentations is a fairly arduous task for everyone involved, and it will assist enormously to plan and communicate intentions as far as possible. As a guide it is suggested that the presentation process for each proposal/design practice should be given a duration of 1.25 hours, with presentations spaced 1.5 hours apart. This implies that a maximum of four presentations per day is desirable. This factor alone may determine how many design consultants should be shortlisted, as the cost associated with several senior client representatives attending a second or third day of presentations will in most cases be prohibitive.

The day should therefore be divided as follows:

Client briefing and pre-meeting preparation	9.00 a.m. to 9.30 a.m.
Presentation 1 and client assessment	9.30 a.m. to 11.00 a.m.
Presentation 2 and client assessment	11.00 a.m. to 12.30 p.m.
Lunch and discussion	12.30 p.m. to 1.30 p.m.
Presentation 3 and client assessment	1.30 p.m. to 3.00 p.m.
Presentation 4 and client assessment	3.00 p.m. to 4.30 p.m.
Conclusion and client decision	4.30 p.m. to 5.30 p.m.

The guidelines should be adjusted as required to suit project scale and/or complexity.

Agenda and structure

This structure of the presentations should be explicitly stated at the outset of the meeting. To guide each consultant an agenda should be circulated at each presentation session. Although the underlying structure of the presentation session is formal, as the information to be gleaned must be consistently collated and assessed, it may none the less be given the sense of a team gathering without sending confusing signals, if the holistic client team approach is explained to the attendees.

The agenda to guide the presentation meeting is given below with an indication of times for each element.

		Time allocated	Time overall
Introductions	by client	5 min.	5 min.
Presentation	by design consultant	15–25 min.	20–30 min.
Questions	by client	20 min.	40–50 min.
Questions	by design consultant	0–5 min.	40–55 min.
Conclusion	by client	0–5 min.	40–60 min.
Post-presentation analysis and preparation for next presentation	by client	20 min.	60–80 min.

Following introductions, the presentation process may be started by requesting that the design practice's lead representative begin by outlining the design philosophy of the practice's work generally, followed by the design philosophy they are bringing to the design of the project. Beyond this point it is up to the consultants to put their design forward in the most appropriate manner, but by this stage a platform of sympathetic team support has been put in place by the client.

Following the presentation of a design practice concept, the client will wish to hold a previously agreed question session to clarify any issues that are unclear or have not been addressed. While it is not possible to list all the headings that this will entail, as they will vary from client to client and project to project, some key headings will inevitably crop up. The questions may be guided by giving each of the client representatives in attendance a time slot for questions/comments relating to their area of professional concern. The tender submission of the report aspect of each design proposal in advance of the presentation date will aid the compilation of questions, which may include consideration of the following:

- Aspects of design philosophy/approach/detail
- Particular areas of operational concern
- Financial analysis of designer's proposals
  - Project costs
  - Project cost control
  - Project management
  - Fees
  - Expenses
- Programme
- AOB.

Presentation evaluation form

Evaluation of each of the design practices' proposals should be carried out immediately following each presentation, even where a presentation session has overrun. A proforma evaluation sheet must be used for this purpose and the evaluation criteria should be agreed by all client attendees and approved by the board of management before the presentation.

As a basic guide, the headings used in Chapter 4 to shortlist the design consultants are to some extent repeated here, although a change in emphasis and detail is required to reflect the focus on evaluation of the designers' response to the project brief rather than the design consultants' general qualities/track record/perceived suitability for the project.

The scoring should be carried out using a combination of intuitive responses to the information given during the presentation, and to the design consultants' tender report document containing the design concept and programme analysis, budget analysis, project management proposals, design team information, fee proposal and so on.

The headings used in the evaluation form should echo the requirements stated within the client design brief.

Where project complexity and/or legislation requires, an evaluation methodology that has legitimacy is provided by the Construction Industry Board.[1]

The CIB methodology, which is endorsed by The National Audit Office, the Audit Commission for England and Wales, the Accounts Commission for Scotland and the Chief Local Government Auditor for Northern Ireland, is based on recommendations from the 1994 *Constructing the Team* report by Sir Michael Latham.[2]

The CIB methodology suggests assessing practices on the general criteria and relative weighting shown in Table 5.1.

Table 5.1   General criteria and relative weighting

Criteria	Suggested weighting range (%)
Practice or company	20–30
Project organisation	15–25
Key project personnel	30–40
Project execution	20–30

The CIB methodology also suggests applying the quality/price ratios for assessing differing types and complexity of project (Table 5.2 on page 76).

The evaluation form (Figure 5.2) has been prepared as a guide for assessing the design practice proposals. The main headings of the form are laid out with a less mathematically involved evaluation system in mind and a focus more plainly on the actual response to the client design brief.

The headings given in the evaluation form are discussed individually so that all the factors in each are considered more comprehensively.

Scoring should be carried out on an individual basis by each client representative, including the project director at the presentation. Each heading should be scored from

Table 5.2   Project types and quality/price ratios

Project type	Quality/price ratio	
	Quality (%)	Price (%)
Feasibility studies	85	15
Innovative projects	80	20
Complex projects	70	30
Straightforward projects	50	50
Repeat projects	20	80

1 to 10 and a total given. The project director or his representative should then complete a final scoring sheet based on taking an average of the marks for each heading given by the individuals within the group. Where appropriate, the weighting system recommended in the CIB guidelines may be more literally implemented to calculate the overall best offer. Whatever the final methodology, the intention is to apply appropriate, consistent and objective criteria to all the proposals.

THE EVALUATION PROCESS

The evaluation of a range of different design proposals is not an altogether straightforward task. Each individual reviewing a design concept will have differing criteria for judging, and many aspects of the design process, certainly the visual and other intellectual aspects, are subjective. The use of a scoring system overcomes this to some extent, although it does not solve every problem. However, although imperfect, it is undoubtedly the only objective, inclusive way forward. The remainder of this chapter discusses the headings given in the evaluation form opposite, noting issues for each heading which it will be worthwhile to consider before marking is under way.

Understanding of the brief/client's business

The first issue to consider when evaluating a design is how well the designers have understood the brief. This may be entirely obvious from their design proposals, or it may require further probing. It is possible to use imagery in drawings that evokes excitement but actually conceals a lack of substance; therefore continual iteration between objective and subjective analysis of a proposal is required. A written statement of design principles will enable a rounded assessment. For example, the conceptual design principles prepared by a design practice for a writers museum began by describing the key relationships identified between the collection of artefacts, physical

Criteria	Design practices 1 (low) 10 (high)			
	A	B	C	D
Understanding of brief/client's business				

Design
   Design concept/approach
   Creativity of the concept
   Aesthetics/materials employed
   Planning/pragmatics/workability of concept
   Operational issues				

Design team experience
   The practice
   Personnel				

Teamworking qualities and communication skills				
Budget analysis				
Programme analysis				

Fee structure
   Fee
   Expenses				

Resources				

Project management
   Project management
   Budget management
   Contract management/administration
   Design management (creativity/pragmatics)				

References Insurance Financial Status				
Total				

Figure 5.2   Evaluation form for design practice proposals

planning options, interpretative planning approaches, lighting and the design response to the existing architectural context. Links between the design principles and key aspects of the client's design brief were also outlined. Following on from the insight provided by the design principles document and its clear relationship to the brief, the plan and visuals presented were therefore more readily and deeply understood by the client organisation. The design principles or design philosophy should clearly arise from the client's business requirements/brief and not simply from a search for conceptual stimuli. A related matter is consideration of how well the practice have understood the business of the client organisation. Both issues should be queried until a satisfactory conclusion is reached.

Design

When evaluating the qualitative aspects of a design concept, several headings will be helpful. These are intended to provide a framework for objective consideration of what may otherwise be seen as subjective matters.

Design concept/approach

Taking on board the intellectual references evinced by a design consultant in their design principles provides an excellent way of getting on to the same wavelength as the designers. Exploring the potential of conceptual design routes that may eventually turn out to be not worth pursuing is a valuable process at this stage. It will also serve to strengthen the feeling of appropriateness when identifying the successful conceptual approach. Since the intellectual approach will determine the aesthetic properties of the design in terms of materials used and the general distribution of elements within the design, it is often possible to gauge the likely success of a design direction in matching a client's requirements from reading the design philosophy alone.

Some general points for consideration of the design philosophy are:

- From what points of reference does the design consultant's concept arise?
- How consistently is this applied to defining subsequent aspects of the concept design? Is this appropriate/successful?
- Do the intellectual references made seem appropriate to the client's project or business aims?
- Do these references add value, that is, do they express the spirit of the client's own vision *and* take it in new and valuable directions?

Creativity of the concept

Depending on the scale, complexity and scope of the project, evaluate the originality of the design response. Does it borrow from other work or is it original? Is it an innovative approach that may provide solutions to more detailed or problematic aspects of the project? Is the design strategy an appropriate fit with the business strategy? What risk is involved? For example a client organisation undertaking a space planning design for an open plan office using standard office furniture systems will be seeking the safe and controlled development and execution of a pragmatic scheme rather than introduce any unnecessary risk through the introduction of innovative and untried ideas. In contrast the design teams working on the building envelope and the exhibitions for the Millennium Dome project were driven by the client's desire to produce innovative design solutions at all levels.

Aesthetics/materials employed

The aesthetic qualities of a design will, or should, arise from the intellectual design approach. They should feel 'right' for the project and the organisation and should express an image that enhances both. In an attempt to make the subjective judgment of visual criteria objective, ask whether the visual imagery matches the client's aspirations for the project: does the design concept visually embody what the brief aspires to? For example, is it 'efficient?', 'cutting edge?', 'traditional?', 'exciting?', 'restful?', 'contemporary?', 'friendly?', 'small business?', 'large corporate entity?' and so on.

Part of judging the visual imagery will require consideration of the types of materials and finishes proposed for the manufacture and construction of the design concept. Even at concept stage the palette of materials and finishes indicated by a designer as appropriate will speak volumes about the underlying concept and the visual qualities of the design approach. Ideally at presentation stage a board of the key finishes and materials proposed will be made available.

Planning/pragmatics/workability of concept

The planning aspects of a project – often termed 'general arrangement' – must be viewed from several different perspectives. A general arrangement that satisfies the strategic needs of the client design brief must be established in principle, before moving into the planning of detailed requirements. At the presentation stage, then, the planning indicated will only be in 'outline' or 'zoning', with activities generally allocated to areas of the building, interior or site. This zoning is, however, fundamental to both the visual qualities of the scheme and to the functionality of the scheme.

Some issues to consider are: does the overall zoning indicated match the functional requirements with the visual qualities desired – that is, open plan, cellular, correct balance of private and public space? Correct balance of activities within the zones? Correct relationships for operational function? What are the operational implications of the zoning plan indicated – from an energy management perspective? From a security perspective? From a health and safety perspective? From a psychological perspective? And so on. What are the maintenance implications of the zoning plan indicated?

Operational issues

Ideally the operational consequences of developing a design proposal should be examined for unforeseen problems or issues before acceptance. This will require input from all client representatives. For example, does a design proposal raise any unforeseen maintenance issues? Financial issues? Personnel issues? Security issues? Health and safety issues? Logistical issues? Have the new operational parameters been sufficiently established by the client to permit evaluation of the design? Has the design been sufficiently developed by the practice to permit evaluation of the operational issues?

Design team experience

There are two main perspectives that merit consideration here: first, the experience and track record of the practice; and second, the experience and track record of the personnel within the design consultants' team.

As regards the practice, does it have direct or transferable experience of the nature, scale and complexity of the project proposed? Is the experience recent? Have any clients had difficulties or disputes with the practice? Who? Why? What was the outcome? References can be checked in relation to this point.

As regards the personnel, do they match the practice experience, that is, are they the same personnel that have the direct experience of the practice? The relevance of this will obviously depend on the nature of the project, but it is vital to check for a project of any complexity. It is important to be clear about the identity of the design consultants' lead contact and/or project team leader and the roles of other personnel.

The responses to the two issues noted above should be given within the written report provided by the design practice.

Teamworking qualities and communication skills

If the design consultants' team will be working closely with an in-house client team, a situation that will occur in the majority of cases involving fit-out work, it is important to gain an impression during the interview process of how the consultant/in-house team will work together in future. This will involve intuitive responses to the personalities and working methods/values of the design practice, and the client's impression of how well the consultants' team will work with the client's project team. It will also involve an assessment of the communication skills of the individual personnel and the practice overall.

Budget analysis

The concept design sets out 'a map' of the intended design response to the brief, and contains all the major issues noted above: planning/zoning of activity, distribution and selection of materials and so on. While this conceptual 'mapping out' process looks for the appropriate functional, visual and eventually construction 'connections' which will be brought together to form the new design, it is also essential to set out the relevant financial connections which support the aspirations of the design philosophy. At this stage, since nothing has been agreed with the client organisation, it is clearly not possible to present a detailed financial plan that answers all questions in detail. The financial information should, however, set out an elemental cost plan that grows from and underpins the design approach, and it should be possible to gain an idea of overall structural financial targets that lie within the conceptual approach.

One important measure at this stage, with regard to the budget analysis provided in the design philosophy report, is the degree of importance placed on budget analysis by the design consultant. Ideally the elemental cost plan will have been prepared by a quantity surveyor as part of the practice's preferred design team. The design practice should be asked to describe the methodology for developing the design solution and managing the coordinated development of the cost plan.

Budget headings given within this section of the design concept proposal will vary depending on the scale of the project. However, as a guide, even with the concept design information at this earliest of stages, it is possible to set out an elemental cost plan using the following typical headings where applicable:

Demolition — Demolition of existing works and removal from site

Substructure — Excavation, foundations and associated works such as new drain and so on. Structural floors, walls and roof

Primary elements — External doors, windows, interior elements such as partitioning, doors and ceilings

Secondary elements — Ceiling, wall and floor finishes. Finishes to other features

Finishes — All waste and water services and all mechanical and electrical services such as air conditioning, heating, lighting and so on

Services — Incoming gas and mains electricity and telecoms and data installations. Also multimedia, audio visual video and so on

Installations/Fixtures — Elements such as sanitary ware, reception desks, built-in seating, shelving and so on. Other specialist features, for example glazed office partitions, picture hanging systems

Furnishings — Furniture which must be provided through the contract, including blinds, planting and so on

External works — Landscaping works, car parks, external lighting and so on

Client's requirements — Any particular needs arising from the client's operation, such as security, fire protection requirements and so on

Contingencies — Depending on the nature of the design project, that is, routine or innovative, a sum of between 5 per cent and 15 per cent should be allowed

Fees and expenses — Discussed further on page 82

Depending on the scale, nature and complexity of the project, these headings may be given for the entire project, or they may be given for separate elements of the project such as Building 1, Building 2 or Ground Floor, First Floor and so on.

Programme analysis

An integral part of the conceptual design proposal linked to both the intended design approach and the elemental cost plan is the design practice response to the timetable set out within the client design brief. The programme, though provisional due to lack of dialogue at this stage, should provide further insight into the consequences of pursuing the design strategy proposed. Key aspects of any phasing requirements of the client organisation noted in the client design brief should be indicated, and should be integrated convincingly and logically. Key dates for moving from pre-construction to construction periods should be indicated and key dates for the provision of client information/briefing should be included. Critical path relationships should be clear.

The programme information should comprise a Gantt chart and a brief relevant narrative, and the information provided should permit informed dialogue to take place. Depending on the scale, nature and complexity of the project, several levels of Gantt chart and narrative may be required, where, for example, a masterplan strategy is being considered for a large greenfield site.

Fee structure

The main criterion that any client seeks in evaluating a fee proposal is value for money. This obviously relates to the qualitative aspects of the design concept proposal and personnel, but it also relates to the quantity of resources being provided over the duration of the project.

Another key area is the completeness of the fee proposal; that is, are any exclusions made or alluded to, and on what basis are expenses estimated?

Fee

An initial checklist for comparing the fee proposals is given in Figure 5.3.

The fee should also be analysed by 'RIBA Plan of Work' stages, as this relates the fee to progress and resources over time. The 'RIBA Plan of Work' is the subject of Chapter 9.

The extent of financial analysis to be carried out must always respond to the scale, nature and complexity of the project. It is possible to produce a surfeit of information that goes beyond the limits of being useful. The recommended course of action is to consider the issues noted above and to include a specified format for preparing fee information within the client design brief so that reasonably direct comparisons between practice responses may be made.

Evaluating expenses

Evaluating expenses is a difficult area for all parties, including the design practice when preparing their proposal. Expenses cannot be estimated with accuracy, although experience will be a reasonable guide. It is certainly worth taking the time to analyse expenses, however, as it at least provides a chance of identifying any obvious misunderstandings, omissions or hidden fees/costs.

Item	Design practice			
	A	B	C	D
Overall fee				
Overall expenses				
Total				
% of contract costs				
Overall resources provided (FTE days)				
Cost per day (average)				

Figure 5.3   Checklist for comparing fee proposals

The headings under which expenses will fall relate generally to key areas such as travel, printing, sustenance, mail, phone and so on. Expenses will depend on geographical factors as well as the nature, scale and complexity of the project, together with any particular requirements that the client may have stipulated. For example, if a London-based design practice is appointed for a major building project in Glasgow or Edinburgh, the client organisation's requirements may include the establishment of a local office for the duration of the project. Where the London practice are competing with local practices, a financial disadvantage is clearly created. The scale of the project and/or the scale of the practice will determine the extent of this disadvantage.

A key aspect of achieving a realistic expenses agreement relates to the management and accounting process to be employed and the basis of the charge. The method of charging for expenses should be 'charged at cost', and copies of invoices should be submitted with all applications for payment of expenses. For some organisations, such as local authorities, the rates of expenses will be predetermined.

Compiling a checklist (Figure 5.4) permits not only a basis for direct comparison but also a check for omissions and a more detailed understanding of the issues affecting each design practice in delivering their services. The purpose of this analysis is not simply to save money at the micro level but to ensure that, whichever practice is selected, no surprises await either party.

Expenses item	A	B	C	D
Overall estimate				
Travel				
Mail				
Printing				
Sustenance				
Phone/fax				
Clients stipulated requirements				
Charged at cost?				
% mark up?				
Concerns				
Total				

Figure 5.4   Expenses checklist

Once again, it is easily possible to over-analyse expenses. The client organisation and design practice should agree a basis for expenses which permits adequate resourcing for the project as required.

Resources

Depending on the scale of the project, the analysis of resources given in Figure 5.5 on page 85 will also be of use.

Project management

The term 'project management' is typically used to describe vague types of activity in rather loose terms. For the purposes of reviewing the project management capabilities of each design practice being interviewed, project management is split here into distinct activities. There are four related aspects of overall project management experience and capabilities that are required from a lead design consultant to ensure the delivery of a satisfactory design process. Without these management capabilities, little or no controlled progress will be achieved. Each should be outlined in the design practice's report and queried during the presentation/interview.

Item	A	B	C	D
Resource provided (director/partner)				
Resource provided (associate)				
Resource provided (senior designer)				
Resource provided (designer)				
Resource provided (technician)				
Resource provided (admin.)				
Resource provided at client's base/site (number of visits)				
% of fee by design discipline • Architects/lead designer • Interior/exhibition designers • Graphic designer • Lighting designer's fee • Others, depending on project • Quantity surveyor's fee • Structural engineer's fee				
Exclusions noted (list any)				
Areas of concern				
Total resources				

Figure 5.5   Analysis of resources

Project management

In this analysis project management refers to the ability of the design practice to 'run a job'. This means chairing site meetings, preparing minutes and inspecting works on site to assess their accordance with the contract documents. It is the ability to communicate progress and problems on site (and off site where manufacture is taking place) and to ensure solutions are found and progress is maintained.

Budget management

The design practice must convincingly present a methodology for maintaining the approved budget during the design development stages. Their reporting methodology should be specified, as should their working methodology with the quantity surveyor, and the two-way information management process explained. For large projects, examples of proposed standard format cost reports should be provided. The methodology for budget management during the construction phase should be specified.

Contract management/administration

Contract management and administration capabilities relate to knowledge of and experience of the types of 'works package' contracts and contract processes envisaged for the project. This links in part to the ability and aptitude of the practice to prepare comprehensive working drawings and specifications, but also to knowledge of differing contract formats and to the relevant contract administration processes. Good contract administration abilities are essential to achieving a successful design process. The design practice will work with the quantity surveyor on these aspects, but must have their own clear and distinct capabilities.

Design management

The design management capabilities required from a lead consultant refer to the ability to coordinate and integrate the design input of other consultants – structural engineers, mechanical and electrical engineers, lighting designers, landscape designers, graphic designers, audiovisual designers and so on – into the design strategy aesthetically, technically and dimensionally and also to drive the design process forward. Design management also refers to the ability to prepare comprehensive packages of tender information such that when a cost is received for a tender item the drawings and specifications and hence the price should be complete.

References

The references provided by each design practice, as requested in the client design brief, should be checked by a member of the client organisation and a brief written report given to the project director. Client organisation staff present at the presentation/interview should be given a copy.

Insurance

The copies of insurance certificates provided by each design practice, as requested in the client design brief, should be checked for compliance with the brief by a member of the client organisation and a brief report given to the project director. Client organisation staff present at the presentation/interview should be given a copy.

Financial status

The copies of financial accounts requested in the client design brief should be sent to the client organisation finance department or another source of financial advice for analysis.

NOTIFYING UNSUCCESSFUL CONSULTANTS

As with the previous process – shortlisting consultants (Chapter 4) – following on from the presentation/interview process it is good practice for the project director to notify unsuccessful design practices and to thank them for their work.

NOTES

1. Construction Industry Board, *Selecting Consultants for The Team: Balancing Quality and Price*, London: Thomas Telford Publishing, 2000.
2. Latham, Sir Michael (1994) *Constructing the Team*, HMSO.

6   Appointment of design consultants

PURPOSE

The purpose of this chapter is to outline the steps necessary to formally confirm the appointment of the successful design practice and other project consultants. It includes discussion of the nature of contracts between clients and their consultants to aid the composition of a bespoke form of appointment. Appropriate legal advice should always be sought when writing any contract, but the first step, as for a design project, is to be clear about what you hope to achieve by writing a brief.

OUTLINE

- Introduction
- Contract law
- Purpose of a form of appointment contract
- Writing a bespoke contract
- Contracts for different professional disciplines
- Signing contracts.

INTRODUCTION

Standard form of appointment contracts are available from most of the professional bodies representing any professional discipline, and are a good starting-point for writing a bespoke contract as most of the individual, fundamental process issues will already have been addressed. However, before considering the writing of a contract in detail, it is essential to be clear about what the contract is intended to achieve in relation to the client organisation and project-specific requirements. Approached in this way, it is reasonably simple for a client to write the brief for a form of appointment contract leaving the exact wording and formatting to a legal adviser. If resources do not permit the input of a legal adviser, then at least a reasonably robust and pragmatic document will have been prepared. There are a number of helpful books available, via RIBA, Building Centre and other bookshops, that provide detailed advice on contract law and management.

CONTRACT LAW

Advice in this book is not a substitute for legal advice but sets out a pragmatic framework for client organisations to use to establish exactly what they wish the contract to achieve. This will provide a clear brief for a legal adviser to prepare appropriate contract documentation with maximum clarity and effectiveness and minimum subsequent input.

There are many forms of contract, depending on the requirements of the parties and the scope of the project. More complex projects call for a number of interdependent documents setting out the agreement in considerable detail. The form of the document is less important than the content: it is desirable to be as clear and as comprehensive as possible in the circumstances.

A contract arises whenever one party makes an offer, which is accepted by the other party, to provide work or services in return for payment or other consideration (which can be nominal, as in the case of work for charity). An agreement does not have to be in writing to form a contract, but to avoid any misunderstanding or failings of memory, it is strongly recommended that details of the agreement are recorded in writing and agreed between the parties.

It should be remembered that a contract will arise as soon as agreement is reached (which may be over the telephone or at a meeting). The details should be settled before the work actually starts; any agreed changes will then become variations to the contract and should also be recorded in writing.

As laws affecting contracts vary from country to country, legal advice should always be taken, especially when working for clients overseas. Contracts should make clear which country's law will govern the operation of the agreement.

PURPOSE OF A FORM OF APPOINTMENT CONTRACT

The purpose of a written contract in general terms is to state explicitly the terms of agreement between two parties 'for the avoidance of any doubt'.

The purposes of a contract for a design project, from a client's perspective, are:

- To make clear the services which are expected from the design consultant
- To make clear the method of delivery of the services required from the design consultant
- To make clear the quality and quantity of resources required from the design consultant and the distribution or delivery of those resources
- To set out the fee agreed for the services
- To set out the expenses agreed for the project
- To set out a schedule of fee payment stages
- To set out the agreed timescale for the delivery of the services
- To set out particular client requirements such as ownership of intellectual property, confidentiality, types and levels of insurance required, control over publicity and other matters related to the project

- To set out a methodology for negotiating variations to the contract by either party, including, for example, cancellation of the project before completion or change of ownership or cessation of trading by one or other party
- To set out a methodology for resolving any disputes which may arise during the project using a form of law applicable to the locality/country of the client/project (English law, Scottish law and so on).

If these issues are satisfactorily resolved by a client organisation and their advisers, and written into explicit terms of a contract, then any risk of a major misunderstanding will already have been minimised. Clearly the aspiration of all parties to a contract is that once it is agreed and signed, neither party will have to look at the contract again. However, if things do change or go wrong it will be impossible to agree a route forward without the framework which a pre-negotiated and agreed arrangement provides.

All design contracts need to cover the same broad elements. For the more complex projects typical of the built environment, the form of appointment contract can be split into three basic components:

1 Form of appointment
2 Conditions of engagement
3 Appendices (of which there may be several).

All three components must be cross-referenced. Each is outlined in more detail below. Ideally the form of appointment contract and the conditions of engagement that a client will use for a project should be available for consultants to consider at briefing stage so that their fee proposal is based on the contract terms, thus avoiding subsequent negotiation.

Figure 6.1, opposite, suggests how the various components may be organised hierarchically to provide a comprehensive form of appointment contract. Generic templates for a form of appointment contract, conditions of engagement and appendices cover sheet based on the following text are included at the end of this chapter. These templates should be completed by the client's design manager and are then submitted to a legal adviser for comment before being signed.

1 The form of appointment contract

Parties to the contract

The contract should start by defining the names and addresses of the parties to the contract.

The project

The name, nature and location of the project should be stated. If the project is to be completed for a fixed budget overall, this should be explicitly stated here. It should also be made clear what this budget includes, that is, all works, including all fees, expenses

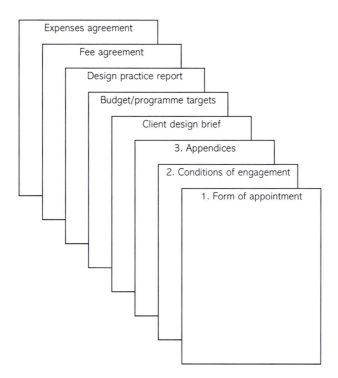

Expenses agreement

Fee agreement

Design practice report

Budget/programme targets

Client design brief

3. Appendices

2. Conditions of engagement

1. Form of appointment

Figure 6.1   Hierarchy of components of a form of appointment contract

and other associated costs. Normal practice is to list all financial figures excluding VAT. Any deviation from this normal practice is likely to lead to confusion.

The agreement

The intended legal and business relationship between the parties should be defined, for example, 'The client organisation appoints the consultant to provide design/ engineering/project management services ...'.

Reference should be made to any supporting material, such as the conditions of engagement, plus appendices such as the client design brief, consultant's proposal document and so on. Where required to provide absolute clarity, key aspects of the agreement may be extracted from the client design brief and/or designer's proposal as separate appendices for separate signing. These might include items such as the agreed cost plan, fee payable, fee payment stages, expenses and so on. It should be noted that all such separate documents are signed and appended to the contract as such, with an appendix cover sheet. Alternatively a schedule of contract documents may be prepared and appended to the contract with only the schedule requiring signatures.

Fees agreed for the services

There are two related aspects of remuneration for professional services to be considered and explicitly recorded within the form of appointment contract: fees and expenses.

Fees

The fee to be paid for the services and the level of variability should be clearly stated within the contract. The fee may be a percentage of the approved contract costs, in which case the final account fee will not be known precisely until the final accounts for works packages are known. Alternatively the fee may be a fixed sum. Obviously the fixed sum gives a client more financial certainty, and from a client's perspective is probably the preferred mode. One suggestion that may be followed is that the fee, originally based on a percentage of the client's anticipated contract expenditure, should be used as a basis of negotiation with the design practice and then agreed as a fixed-sum fee; or the fee may be a fixed sum based on a resource provision and daily/hourly rate for different team members (see section on Additional services). For some types of consultancy work, particularly shorter-duration projects such as feasibility studies and the like, it is common to quote a fee in daily rates, and state a given number of days.

Expenses

The expenses anticipated for a project can be explicitly built into the contract in a number of ways depending on the scale and nature of the project. It is obviously in a client's interest to agree a maximum limit on the expenditure of expenses; however, this may not be possible and will depend on the absence of any unquantified variables. The more precise the client design brief and project methodology, the more accurate the estimates of expenses will be.

In a straightforward small-scale project with a local design practice, for example, the expenses will for the main part cover printing, post, phone/fax and couriers. There may be limited or even no travel expenses. A larger-scale project with a design practice based outside the locality of the client organisation and/or project will require a more detailed analysis of the expenses. Establishment of a local office and/or substantial travel may be required. Expenses for substantial travel, subsistence costs/overnight stay may be involved.

Where straightforward, expenses may be agreed in advance and become a fixed element of the fee within the contract, giving one less process to be managed during the project. This also has the advantage of making the design practice responsible for managing the expenses. Client organisations may also choose to ensure that expenses are incurred only on an 'out-of-pocket' basis, with invoices submitted. In conjunction with setting a maximum limit on expenses and monthly measurable targets on expenses, this route provides maximum client control, although it is another process to be managed.

It is important to balance the desire to 'fix and forget' the overall fee, including expenses, as a single package with the desire to exercise management control over every detail. The final decision will rest with the nature and scale of the client and the project.

Personnel

The key personnel to be provided by the design practice in support of the services and their project role – partner, project designer, assistant and so on – should be specified in the contract.

Other issues

Other issues to include within the form of appointment include project-specific issues that the client wishes to draw attention to, such as the relationship with other aspects of the business operation/site or liaison with other consultants/staff/projects on a large project, method of delivery, that is, local office to be established where the practice is based remotely, completion date of project/contract and so on.

Signature

Rules governing signature of formal documents depend on the legal nature of the client organisation (for example sole trader, partnership, limited company, local authority) and on national law.

Normally (except in the case of local authorities) the signature of two witnesses is also required. Application of the company seal may be necessary for limited companies.

2 Conditions of engagement

The purpose of the conditions of engagement is to set out the terms of the business relationship between the parties. This includes listing the standard services to be provided and methods for agreeing variations to the contract. Other areas to be covered are, for example, speed of payment by the client, methods for resolving disputes, what happens if the project is postponed or cancelled after the contract is signed and so on. Conditions of engagement may be drawn up for the particular project, or may be standard to the organisations concerned (adapted as necessary to the circumstances of a specific commission).

Services expected from the design consultant

The services required from the design practice during the project will be a mix of professional services which are standard to the delivery of most projects, and those which are specific to the client organisation and project. Each must be articulated appropriately within the conditions of engagement.

Services which are client/project-specific relate either directly to the project requirements or the business operation, including, for example, how the consultant will interface with the client's staff or other in-house specialists during the project. The aim of the conditions of engagement is to ensure that both the standard and the specific services are fully articulated so that both parties have no misunderstandings.

Clauses may be included to ensure that the design of a particular aspect, say incorporation of particular technologies, is specified within the contract. There may be particular requirements to report on progress or obtaining approvals before proceeding, or to provide high levels of detail with regard to particular aspects of the design and so on. Client organisations must prepare their own list of requirements in conjunction with their design manager.

The services which a contract must specify and which may not be so apparent to some client organisations relate to the more generic role within the design and construction team, including aspects such as:

- Definition of the design practice as the lead project consultant (where this is the case) responsible for the coordination of design information produced by other consultants
- The design practice's responsibility to advise the client on the need for other consultants and the level of fee that might be expected
- The works contract strategy, defining the role in terms of working drawings to be produced, tender procedures to be observed, and contract administration duties.

A schedule of standard services may be prepared using a checklist based on the Chartered Society of Designers (CSD) or RIBA services (for addresses see page 174) and should clearly correspond to the plan of work stages and resource plan stated in the form of appointment. A balance of generic and specific *'but not limited to'* service descriptions is required. A design manager will ensure clarity from a client's perspective.

Additional services/variations to the contract

The basis of agreement for any additional services and/or variations from the form of agreement that become required during the project must be stated. It should be clearly specified that a separate agreement to proceed on the basis of any additional services fee must be given by the client in writing before any work is undertaken by the designer. Although hourly rates are often quoted as a basis for additional service fees, negotiation often takes place to agree a fixed sum or ceiling.

It is normal to define a list of hourly rates for additional works within the contract for:

- The director/partner
- Associates
- The senior designer
- The designers
- Technicians
- Administration
- and so on.

These rates may be set out as an appendix or as a part of the fee agreement.

Particular client organisation requirements

The following generic headings are outlined as a basis for developing a set of clauses to permit the particular requirements of specific client organisations to be established.

Confidentiality
Client organisations should explicitly state the standards and level of confidentiality

that they expect from their consultants and/or contractors and from anyone employed by the consultant or contractors. In many cases, such as local authorities or other public-sector clients, this may be governed by the parent organisation. Formal consultation at board of management level is required. These issues will normally also be covered by the Codes of Conduct of professional associations to which consultants customarily belong.

Intellectual property

Client organisations should explicitly state their position regarding intellectual property. Taking legal advice is recommended, as intellectual property is a complex and much-debated topic. There is potential for conflict of interest here between the rights and interests of designers and clients; however, the key issue to bear in mind is that a client will seek to retain ownership of design information and design rights arising from work undertaken on the project to ensure control over factors that might directly or indirectly affect its business. A design practice should not be asked to accept unreasonable terms, and in fact is protected by law in key areas of intellectual property and general contract law, as already noted. The Copyright, Designs and Patents Act 1988 as subsequently amended sets out the UK position, together with legislation covering parallel areas such as patents and trade marks.

This book does not cover intellectual property in great depth since it is such a complex topic in its own right, and is subject to continuous change, other than to note that the key areas of intellectual property include:

- Copyright
- Patents
- Trade marks
- Design registration
- Unregistered design rights
- Moral rights (rights of paternity and integrity).

Continuously updated guidance on intellectual property matters for all parties entering into a design project is available from the Chartered Society of Designers.

Assignment and licence of intellectual property

The ownership of any right can be changed by agreement between the parties entering into a contract. This change of ownership may be outright by 'assigning all rights to *the client organisation*' upon entering into the contract, or rights may be transferred 'on licence' for a mutually agreeable period and on specified terms. An appropriate and equitable agreement should be the aim, and it is easiest to discuss and resolve an agreement in the context of specific business and project requirements.

Third parties

Depending on the nature and complexity of the project, client organisations will also wish to ensure that no breach of any of the above rights already owned by a third party takes place as a consequence of the project. Any design work carried out during the project must be original and must not plagiarise any existing work. The responsibility of the design practice to ensure that no breach takes place should be clearly stated.

Rights in work subcontracted as part of the project will also need to be assigned or licensed to the client organisation. This is normally the responsibility of the contracting body.

Physical materials

There are no legal rights arising from an idea. All the rights noted above rest in the manner in which the ideas are expressed. With this in mind, for the avoidance of doubt, client organisations may wish to state specifically state that all physical materials, drawings, sketches, models and so on produced as a consequence of the project will be owned by, or assigned to, the client organisation or as otherwise agreed.

Provision may also need to be made for the ownership of rights and physical materials arising in any work produced jointly by the consultants and the client organisation (for example, in the development stages of the project).

Insurance

A client should explicitly state the levels of insurance that it expects from its consultant and from anyone employed by the consultant. In many cases, such as local authorities or other public-sector clients, this may be governed by its parent organisation. The client project director or his representative should consult with their board of management on this matter. Types of insurance that may be required include:

- Professional indemnity insurance
- Public liability insurance
- Product liability
- Employers' liability insurance.

If the guidelines within this book have been followed, copies of certificates of insurance held were requested as part of the design practice concept report to protect a client's interests.

Working within the estate of the client organisation

Client organisations must state their security and access management procedures where these will apply to external personnel gaining access to the estate. The procedures for gaining permits of any kind should be specified. Where there will be a requirement for repeat access, each of the consultant's personnel should be treated as 'staff' and given an appropriate 'induction process', with normal hours of access and so on to be determined.

Publicity

Upon completion of a new design project, client organisations will wish to promote and publicise the venture. Similarly the design practice and other consultants/ contractors associated with the project will wish to gain publicity. The extent and terms of such publicity should be agreed in advance. Permission to use photographs and so on should not be unreasonably withheld from any party involved in the venture. Clients may stipulate that in addition to approving any artwork and text for any promotional material before use, a formal credit, using approved text supplied by the client, must be included.

Retention

It is not usual to apply retentions to payment of fees for consultants. Retentions are applied only in works contracts with contractors. They encourage contractors to return to the works at the end of the contract latent defects period to make good defects.

Payment of invoices

Client organisations should specify an appropriate period within which payment will be made to consultants from receipt and certification of invoices. This should reflect an adequate period of time for internal processes to take place but should not exceed 30 days.

Resolving disputes

The contract must explicitly state a method for resolving disputes over the contract. There are several methods available:

- Arbitration – A third-party arbitrator may be pre-agreed in the event of a dispute
- Adjudication – For use where the Housing Grants, Construction and Regeneration Act 1996 applies. Any of the parties to a contract may refer disputes to the adjudicator, who must provide a decision within 28 days. On receipt of a referral the adjudicator may take the initiative in seeking information. The adjudicator's decision is binding
- Conciliation (or negotiation) – To resolve the dispute, the parties follow a pre-agreed conciliation or negotiation procedure, perhaps without any third-party intervention
- Litigation – Any dispute will be dealt with in a court of law. This route for resolution of disputes is not recommended other than as a final resort.

Legal advice should be taken when deciding on the most appropriate method in relation to the nature of the project, the nature of the services being procured and the nature of the organisations involved in the contract.

Termination of contract

The contract should contain a clause that protects the interests of either party in the event of the contract being terminated prematurely.

Duty of care/collateral warranties

Only parties who have entered into a contract have rights and/or obligations under that contract, yet it is often the case that a third party, for example, a purchaser or funding party, has an interest in a project which they wish to protect. A collateral warranty provides a framework for establishing a contractual relationship between a third party and the parties to the 'original contract'. Where appropriate therefore, the requirement for consultants and/or contractors to enter into a collateral warranty should be noted, and the nature of the collateral warranty specified. Standard collateral warranties are available from the British Property Federation.

3 Appendices

The appendices should be organised in a hierarchical manner and should be prefaced by an appendix cover sheet which schedules all the attachments and which is signed and annexed as appropriate.

Client design brief

The first appendix should be the client design brief defining the objectives of the project. It is the foundation of the business interface between the client organisation and the design practice.

Design practice proposal

The design practice response to the client design brief is the agreed approach to achieving the brief. Ideally any alterations will be made to this document before inclusion within the appendices.

Schedule of fee payment stages

Since fee payment stages are likely to be expressed as tied in to individual projects, this item is included within the appendices to a contract. As such it is explicitly signed by both parties, making clearer the agreement.

Depending on the nature of the contract, fees may be paid in regular equal instalments or upon achieving key stages of the project. Where the professional relationship is untried, the fee stages should be tied to the completion of key stages, not to dates. This minimises risk of financial exposure for a client by ensuring payment is formally linked to achievement. Standard stages of achievement are stated with the RIBA Plan of Work. Alternatively clients may write their own key stages of achievement as appropriate to the nature of their business.

Where an ongoing professional relationship has been established or where a consultant is engaged on a retainer basis, fees may be paid in regular equal instalments. Clients can expect to receive some negotiation and 'input' from consultants on the matter of fee payment stages and any proposal must be fair to both parties.

Resources required from the design consultant

As part of the presentation stage process outlined earlier in the book, each design practice was requested in the client design brief to provide a map of resources to assist with the evaluation of tender returns. The agreed provision of design, or other consultants' resources for the project should now be explicitly built into the contract. This should include an appropriate level of detail regarding, say, the amount of site attendance and/or direct contact and liaison with the client, which personnel are involved and how the resources are delivered relative to the programme and payment of fees.

Timescale for delivery of the services

The timescale for delivery of the services to be provided may also be included as an appendix to the contract. As such it is explicitly signed by both parties, making clearer the agreement.

WRITING A BESPOKE CONTRACT

The text in this chapter about form of appointment contracts, like the overall text of the book about design project management, is intended to enable client organisations to retain control by providing a full understanding of the process. It is not intended to replace the need for professional legal advice. If the steps for shortlisting, briefing and selecting consultants outlined in the book have been followed, then the contract writing process is already under way. The client will be clear in terms of project intent and will have obtained a clear proposal and methodology from his consultant. It is a reasonably straightforward matter to use the information gained and the methodology laid out in this chapter to set out the contract which binds it all together. It will still help, however, to have a 'draft' contract to refer to.

Legal advice should be taken when turning the briefing information and consultant's response into a contract for a project, to ensure that appropriate language and conventions are used and that the specific project intentions as outlined generically above are consistent and will be recognised in the law of the country which is to apply to the contract.

CONTRACTS FOR DIFFERENT PROFESSIONAL DISCIPLINES

The basic principles set out above for writing a brief for a 'form of appointment for design consultants' apply whatever the professional discipline. However, from a client's perspective of retaining control over the whole process, it is important to be aware of the key areas of service supplied by each discipline. There is no substitute for experience here, particularly in relation to the client organisation's own mode of operation. A shortcut to providing an entirely bespoke contract is to obtain a standard form of appointment contract from the relevant professional body and amend it using the information laid out in this chapter as a guide in conjunction with taking further formal legal advice as required.

Sources of standard form of appointment contracts

- Chartered Society of Designers
  Contracts for appointing Interior Designers, Exhibition Designers, Graphic Designers
- Royal Institute of British Architects
  Contracts for appointing architects (various)
- Royal Institution of Chartered Surveyors
  Contracts for appointing Quantity Surveyors and other surveyor disciplines and for project management
- Royal Town Planning Institute
  No contract at present, but database of registered consultants available
- Association of Consulting Engineers
  Contracts for appointing structural, civil, electrical and mechanical engineers and planning supervisors
- The Landscape Institute
  Contracts for appointing Landscape Architects
- British Property Federation
  Collateral Warranties.

The Design Council website (www.designcouncil.org.uk) and the Construction Industry Council website (www.cic.org.uk) provide web-based links to most of the above organisations and a wide range of other related professional and trade bodies. See also the addresses given at the end of the book (p. 174).

SIGNING CONTRACTS

There are two questions relating to the signing of contracts to be discussed here – 'Who can sign the contract?' and 'How will the completion of signed contracts be achieved logistically?'

Who can sign?

We have already noted that rules governing signature are dependent on the legal form of the organisations entering into the contract. The personnel who sign the contract from each organisation must therefore have the legitimate authority of their organisation to do so.

How will the completion of signed contracts be achieved logistically?

A signed original of the contract is required for each party to the contract. A meeting may be arranged at which the requisite personnel from each organisation attend, sign and leave, each with a signed original. Alternatively the client may issue two unsigned sets of the contract to the other party with a covering letter requesting that both be signed and returned. It is advisable to include with the covering letter a schedule of pages within the contract documentation that require signatures. Upon receipt the client should sign both originals, keep one, and return one fully signed original to the other party.

Record keeping

In either situation outlined above for the contract signing process, a covering letter from the client design manager should record the exchange of the signed contract documents.

Where appropriate, a contract register (Figure 6.2) may be maintained by the client organisation to track contracts entered into.

Originals of signed contracts including all bound schedules and appendices should be safely filed – with a solicitor if this is felt appropriate.

No.	Date	Project	Consultant/Contractor	Services	Sum	File located
1						
2						
3						
4						

Figure 6.2   Example of a contract register

7 Design development, design coordination and information management

PURPOSE

The purpose of this chapter is to outline the steps necessary to develop the concept design to successful completion on a team-wide basis. It describes the communication and management systems required to address the difficulties that may arise during the design development process, and outlines the range of communication interfaces that are established between client organisations and their design team during the life of the project. It considers the reporting requirements that client organisations should specify to ensure controlled progress and suggests structures to support this communications process in a way that permits iteration and control in equal measure. The chapter uses brief case studies to illustrate the issues.

OUTLINE

- Introduction
- How to judge successful design development
- What is design coordination? Design management?
- Balancing client and consultant aspirations
- Hierarchy, power and professional relationships
- Formats for reporting progress – balancing aspirations and minimising conflict.

INTRODUCTION

This chapter is about client-focused design management. It is also about team-building and leadership, and communicating and maintaining the clear intent of the client design brief during an iterative design development process which may call for or suggest change. It outlines the importance of clients taking the lead and suggests communication and reporting methodologies for achieving this. The text is based on experience and observation and examines where and why conflict may arise, and how to manage it.

HOW TO JUDGE SUCCESSFUL DESIGN DEVELOPMENT

Successful design development should have two fundamental and obvious goals – a successful design solution and a successful design process. As we have touched upon at various points in the text, however, neither of these can be taken for granted. Achieving either, never mind both, requires effective design management and coordination.

The value of achieving a successful design solution is obvious; that of achieving a successful design process is no less obvious, as an inevitable relationship is clear. However, in practice the design process is too often neglected, perhaps in the hope that it will 'self-manage', given that a range of experienced professionals from both within and outside the client organisation have been appointed. Although it is possible to reach a successful design solution with a design process that is less than perfect, this will probably lead to frustration and a waste of resources and opportunity for all concerned.

Design development is the process that synthesises the client design brief with the design solution in a way which should make it appear that a single obvious and successful step has been taken from one to the other. The process should permit a full exploration of creative beneficial options while allowing control to be maintained.

The design development process involves understanding and coordinating the progression of briefing, aesthetic development, intellectual development, technical development, financial control and programme control simultaneously. The successful design development process therefore requires design coordination of all the above to achieve the appearance of this 'single step' despite an often amorphous reality for many of the contributors (Figure 7.1).

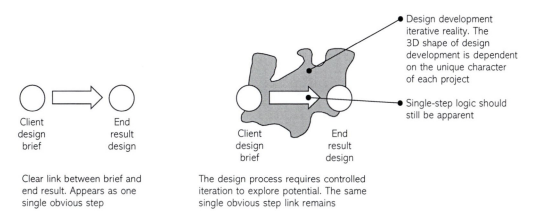

Figure 7.1   The shape of design development

WHAT IS DESIGN COORDINATION? DESIGN MANAGEMENT?

Design coordination might be described in a general way as the management of creative intent. In part it is one of the functions most usually carried out by the lead design consultant on a project. In the context of aesthetic and technical design it demands establishing an initial design framework for all the other design disciplines. It then involves the lead consultant in checking all design and production information to ensure that the designs for (say) lighting or air conditioning all work within the master design and that there are no conflicts either visually or physically. While this is no easy matter, particularly on a large project with complex and conflicting physical requirements for mechanical and electrical services, structure and finishes, it is obvious that the lead consultant has clear criteria against which to assess and coordinate the designs of others – his own design framework.

It is also obvious that the task facing a lead consultant would be all the more onerous if any of the sub-consultants involved in producing design information did not fully understand the design framework set out by the lead consultant – or did not possess the skills necessary to draw up their own design! It would also be difficult to control if any of the sub-consultants did not recognise the need to revise their initial designs following submission to the lead designer in order to coordinate with the overall design effort.

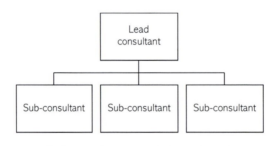

Design coordination on a buildings contract

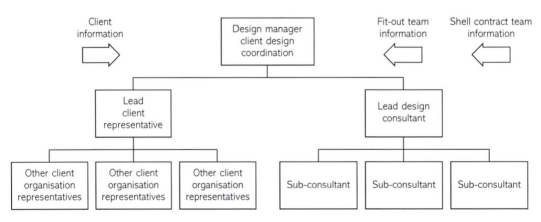

Design coordination on a fit-out contract
requires design management

Figure 7.2   Different needs for design management

This situation is unlikely to occur to any marked degree where individual professional consultants are appointed on a speculative project; however, during fit-out design projects in particular, situations analogous to the above may often arise. Fit-out and interior design work is driven as much by 'business' and the resulting 'people' issues as by technical design issues, and the key difference from a shell or building contract stems from the close interaction of client organisation representatives within the design team framework (Figure 7.2).

Management of the client organisation representative's input to the design process is one of the most valuable aspects of design management, since any uncertainty or unfamiliarity regarding new client operational matters can cause major blockages in the essential two-way flow of information between the brief and the design (Figure 7.3). This is an aspect that sets design management apart from project management and from the design management role of a lead consultant.

Effective client-focused design management requires:

- An understanding of the project brief
- An understanding the design process
- An understanding and empathy with the design intention
- An understanding of the construction process
- An understanding of a client's business at strategic, marketing and operational levels
- An understanding of contract procedures
- Early involvement to establish an appropriate team structure
- An appropriate level of legitimate authority
- Strong administration and communication skills.

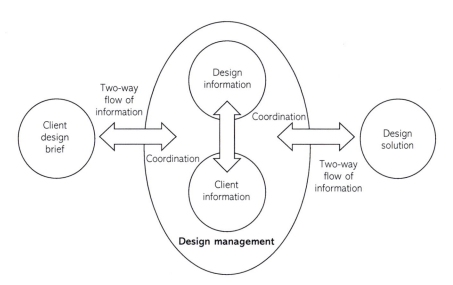

Figure 7.3 The role of design management

Client-focused design management demands the ability to analyse requirements iteratively at macro and micro levels and the legitimate authority to assemble and direct teams and sub-teams in an appropriate and 'open' fashion. It is a process that may be of little value to organisations which undertake repetitive or speculative 'shell' work, where stand-alone construction industry roles and processes will be adequate. Formulaic work for developers is an example. Client-focused design management is of maximum benefit where 'one-off' projects running alongside the continued core operation of a client organisation are planned, in particular where a client's business requirements must be integrated in detail into a project, and where a number of client representative contributors and specialist consultants are assigned to the project.

Design management combines the 'normal project management' role with the design coordination aspect of a lead design consultant role. It must recognise gaps in communications that exist in the project structure and complete the system (Figure 7.4).

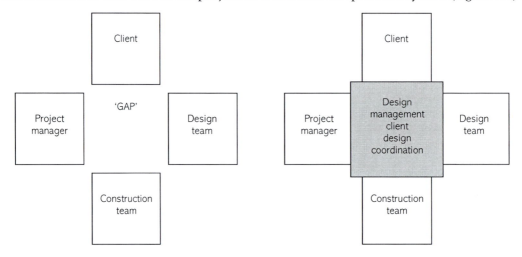

Figure 7.4   Filling the gap in communications

BALANCING CLIENT AND CONSULTANT ASPIRATIONS

One of the most difficult aspects of the design management process is managing the contradiction, complexity and conflict that arise within areas of 'project interface'. 'Project interface' issues arise as a result of overlapping professional concern and interest. The interface issues will change during the life cycle of the project (see Figure 7.5) and may arise from overlapping roles and responsibilities in:

- Briefing (strategic and operational)
- Briefing (between business functions)
- Design responsibility
- Works activity on site
- Cost control
- Project activity/client's business operation and organisation.

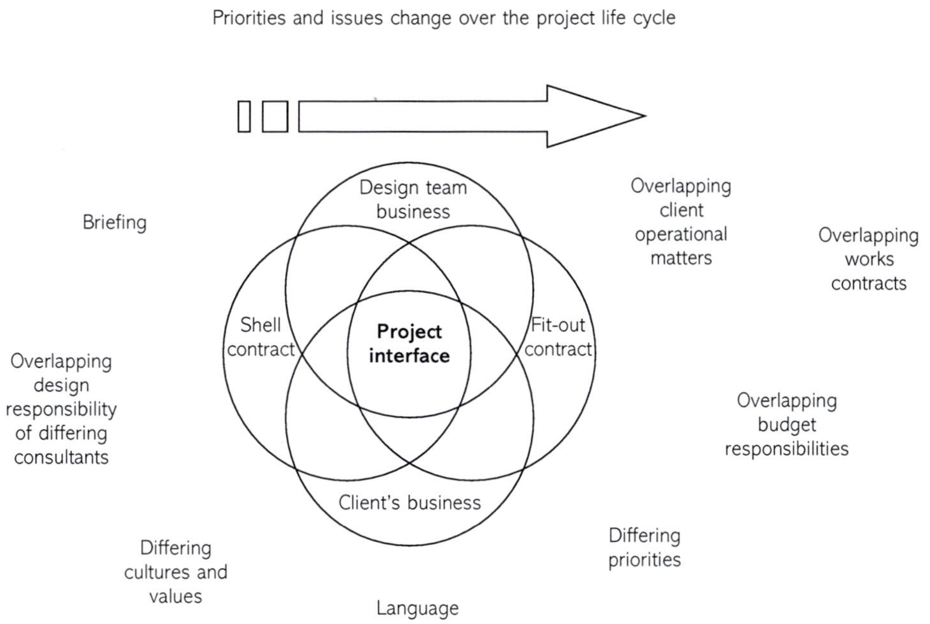

Priorities and issues change over the project life cycle

Design team business

Overlapping client operational matters

Overlapping works contracts

Briefing

Shell contract

Project interface

Fit-out contract

Overlapping design responsibility of differing consultants

Overlapping budget responsibilities

Client's business

Differing priorities

Differing cultures and values

Language

Figure 7.5   Overlapping project issues

Taking the above issues into account, along with the previously discussed communications gap which often exists between designers and clients arising from the differing business sector and organisational culture and so on, it is clear that there is much scope for conflict unless the interface issues are managed appropriately.

For the design manager, any project interface area can be expected to demand three to four times the attention that a stand-alone area of professional concern may require. Some of these project interface headings are explored in more detail below, using some brief case studies.

Design briefing interface

The first project interface to consider is the interface between design and briefing, the major interface area between designers and clients.

A project may make new and untried demands on a client organisation, perhaps taking the client into new areas of operation in terms of geography, technology or even business sector. Typically, then, some aspects of the brief will not be clear to the client even at relatively late stages of the project. This may lead to the requirement, at a late stage, for alterations to aspects of work already carried out, a situation which can lead to frustration and even ill feeling between team members.

Conflicting briefing requirements often arise from a client being, in the words of one designer, 'multi-headed'. The 'multi-headed' client situation may arise where a client comprises more than one organisation, but also where a single client organisation has conflicting interdepartmental interests which have not been resolved. In both instances providing appropriate management and communication requires a suitably experienced design manager without whose direction abortive work is likely to be carried out.

> Graham Russell, Chief Executive Officer of The Northcross Group, notes a museum project for which a dynamic and contemporary design scheme was approved and developed with 'the client', only to be shelved at an advanced design stage because a different part of the client body – a different organisation – voiced concerns. Graham also noted an example where global companies, although a single organisation, may appear as a multi-headed client because of geographically split levels of responsibility. For example, directives from a New York office may radically change the brief for design work that has reached an advanced stage of development based on an initial brief given by a London office.

There will also be occasions where client operational matters make conflicting demands on the brief. Whether these conflicts arise from within the operational fit-out requirements, or between shell contract and fit-out contract requirements, the briefing/design interface issues need careful management to avoid the conflict becoming wasteful or confrontational and to turn it instead into a unique project opportunity.

> Stephen Richards, Development Manager with the National Museums of Scotland, notes a previous experience as a designer. After he was given a brief to design a temporary exhibition for a client of the time, it became clear upon completion of the installation that the space now occupied by the exhibition was also required for part-time catering facilities. This led to consequent changes to the design of the finished installation and to increased cost and time resources required from contributors. A coordinated and comprehensive brief would have provided the opportunity for a unique design solution to ensure the coexistence of both sets of requirements.
>
> In contrast to this situation of unclear and fragmented briefing, Derek Hodgson, Director of Derek Hodgson Associates, Product Designers, notes that his practice usually approach client organisations with an idea for a product which they themselves have developed by studying the marketplace. Often they will then be commissioned to further develop the brief and the design by the client organisations. The development of the brief and the design development are closely linked almost on a partnering basis, an approach which echoes closely some of the recommendations of the Egan Report, 'Rethinking Construction'.[1]

Some of the main briefing/design project interface issues to be dealt with will arise from managing the conflicting design parameters which arise between the architectural design team and fit-out design team responsibilities as noted earlier. Often an architectural design is 'completed' and site works are in progress, managed say by a developer's design team and/or perhaps the client's estates team, and yet the detailed requirements for fit-out are not available from the operator's design team during construction stages. This situation is not untypical.

Kevan Shaw, Director of Kevan Shaw Lighting Design, notes a not untypical situation whereby fit-out requirements will identify a demand for electrical loading for the interior of 35 W/m^2, when the building infrastructure has been designed around a provision of 20 W/m^2. This change in specification of electrical loading may lead to the new requirement for new plant (a substation) at a very late stage, with all the 'knock-on' programme risk, increased cost and aesthetic/statutory consent issues this implies.

David MacRitchie, an associate with Page and Park Architects, notes late briefing information – post completion – for one project leading to the retrospective installation of works to large areas of glazing – a better and more permanent specification for which could easily have been achieved during the construction process for little added cost had the brief been clear.

Design responsibility interface

At the beginning of the book, the differing professional outlook brought by clients, designers and other consultants was explained in terms of respective training, language, professional culture and aspiration. This obviously remains a factor to bear in mind when considering design responsibility through the project interfaces between client and designer or designer and contractor that exist in a variety of ways throughout the project.

Mike Spearman, Managing Director of The Multimedia Team (TMT), notes a variety of overlapping design responsibilities with clients, particularly in the design of multimedia, which can lead to conflicting demands. Personal aspirations of contributors rather than the objectively observed needs of users often influence briefing on behalf of a client organisation. A generic example relates to clients seeking 30 minutes or more of in-depth information while observation and trials indicate that members of the public – the users – will use a maximum of 5–7 minutes, an issue which TMT attempt to resolve during the design development process. Another example relates to the new methods of learning which multimedia and related technologies have presented. A tension is often generated between traditional and new educational opportunities and values when evaluating 'structural' and navigational interface and content issues.

Most project interface difficulties arise where there is an overlapping iterative area of mutual professional concern rather than an area that may be technically developed in isolation. This affects design responsibility issues in particular on large projects with separate building and fit-out design teams. Coordination and continuity of aesthetic 'styling' and structural design responsibilities are likely to provide most scope for overlapping decision-making. Identifying and articulating the problems that must be resolved requires careful design management.

Graham Russell, Northcross, notes one large permanent exhibition project where the director of the client organisation was replaced on three occasions, during which time changes were made to the building design by the architectural design team without consideration of the consequences for the interior design. No communication relating to the change took place until the fitting-out began. The result was a completed design with needlessly unresolved visual aspects.

During a major Scottish Museum Project, regular design coordination meetings were held with the project director to coordinate the aesthetic development of elements in which the architectural team, the exhibition's design team and conservation design team had overlapping design responsibilities and interests. These design coordination meetings also ensured that the related design input from a variety of structural engineers was clearly established and agreed on a collective basis.

Kevan Shaw, of Kevan Shaw Lighting Design, notes that coordination of design responsibility and timing of briefing information is vital if abortive work to services-related items is to be avoided, particularly so when separate shell and fit-out design teams are appointed. On a recent project many building design team members were dismayed to note the removal of unused building light fittings as the fit-out design works began on site. The client had not appointed and briefed a fit-out design team until the building was almost complete, removing any possibility of optimised design coordination between the two sets of requirements.

During the manufacture of specialist fit-out elements such as reception desks, display cases, signage, furniture and so on the design responsibility of the design team often overlaps with a degree of design responsibility from the fabrication team, particularly where a manufacturer is customising standard manufactured elements. The ultimate boundaries of design responsibility must be clear not only for reasons relating to structural integrity but also to cost responsibility, as will be noted later.

Following the completion of a new visitor facility, a large and heavy glazed screen with a steel frame crashed from a high level onto the floor. Had anyone been close to the screen at the time it could have caused injury from the breaking and flying glass; anyone directly under the screen could have been killed. The works contract format – a contractor design portion contract – clearly identified the source of design responsibility as the contractor. During the discussions to rectify the situation it became apparent that the contractor had not understood the full extent of their responsibility to complete the design, including, in this case, designing the fixing of the screen to the fabric of the building. This led to a complete review of all the works carried out by the contractor to provide an assurance of structural integrity.

On large-scale projects, there will often be separate works contracts for fit-out work and 'shell' building work and hence an interface between the shell or 'base-build' contract and the 'fit-out' contract, or indeed fit-out contracts. This project interface area has scope for management difficulties arising from all the project interface issues already noted, plus further 'change management' issues.

Conflict can arise due to the overlap of two separate contracts on site when fit-out works begin in a new and empty building which has just achieved, or may be about to achieve, 'practical completion'. As fit-out works commence on site, recent shell contract installations, particularly services installations and finishes work, may require new work to be carried out by the fit-out contractor team. Without strong coordination and communication, it is easy for the shell contractor responsible for the initial works to pass responsibility for any defects on to the fit-out contractor as damage, in effect, potentially removing the defects liability responsibility of the buildings contractor. Particularly clear management and administration of each contractor's movements on site are required to ensure that responsibilities for any damage or defects are auditable during the shell contractor's 'snagging' process, and as the fit-out contractor begins installation in parallel. Any damage caused to works carried out by either contractor may be blamed by each on the other unless good 'neutral' site management is maintained. On a stand-alone several-trades contract similar management may be required where separate trades works overlap, for example light fittings installed by one contractor behind decorative glass by another or vice versa.

> On a waterfront retail development which involved a separate shell main contractor and fit-out main contractor, the shell contractor who had installed the floor and integrated services trunking refused to carry out any remedial defects rectification, blaming the imperfections recorded on the fit-out contractors who had carried out a range of works in the areas noted. A solution was eventually achieved, but at the cost of time and effort on the part of consultants, client and developer's representatives.

Where a buildings contract and a fit-out contract overlap, the cooperation of both contractors is required to ensure smooth operations on site. Where a new contractor is introduced for the fit-out works, although the complication of overlapping defects liability responsibilities is introduced, at least a fresh new team is gained. This can be particularly advantageous if the external building contract has been problematic.

> A new-build museum building shell contract, which achieved practical completion over six months late, had the same main contractor appointed to carry out the fit-out works (as a separately tendered and awarded contract). Initially the same main contractor personnel were on site to service the fit-out works contract. However, the existing 'mind-set' meant that insufficient attention was initially paid to the requirements of the new fit-out contract until new personnel were introduced. Even then, 'mind-set' difficulties continued to prevent the new team from achieving their full potential. Despite the added requirement to closely manage and administer any works affecting defects liability of the shell contractors, the change management advantage of having a fresh fit-out contractor team would have benefited the client organisation and the project efforts overall.

Cost control interface

Management of cost control on a project has scope to create areas of overlapping professional responsibility and hence project interface. These may arise within the design team from design responsibility issues or works responsibility interfaces, or within the client organisation where responsibilities overlap.

Responsibility and accountability for all aspects of cost planning and for cost reporting within the client organisation must be established before any financial commitments are made, and clear responsibilities for management and procurement must be in place if effective management and cost monitoring are to be ensured. This relates to budget responsibilities within the client organisation, and the interrelated budget responsibilities of client organisation staff working on the project. Design team budget responsibilities must also be clearly identified.

A new visitor centre fit-out design team was prevented from achieving clarity of financial reporting due to difficulties in maintaining the new project hierarchy, as the fit-out works took over from the shell contract as the main focus of client organisation attention. Lack of clarity within the client organisation regarding project roles and responsibilities led to confusion for the contractor and the consultants, who became unsure in effect who 'the client' was. An additional design management resource was required at a late stage to resolve the confusion by providing a structure for reporting methodologies. Linked to this briefing issue within the project was a related cost reporting problem within the organisation. Concerned client organisation board of management members sought financial reports from the head of finance rather than directly from the staff project manager who should have been accountable. The head of finance understandably could not provide adequate information as the staff project manager struggled to provide a clear overall report that had credibility.

Responsibility for cost reporting also relates to design and briefing responsibility. Where briefing and/or design responsibility is unclear, responsibility for costs will also be unclear.

Kevan Shaw recalls completing a detailed fit-out lighting scheme design with a client and various fit-out consultants. Installation of the scheme began on site and quickly uncovered steelwork in areas that were not indicated on any shell contract drawings. Moving the steelwork demanded financial and programme resources which were not feasible, but even so, a new lighting design scheme was required, with additional fees, repairs to the areas of building which had opened up, light fittings to be returned to the manufacturer, some others requiring customisation, and some replacement fittings were required – but who was responsible for the communications gap and the consequent disruption, delay and associated cost? No one had been appointed to coordinate both sets of criteria and each designer had designed within independent original client briefs.

Project activity/client's business operation interface

The project activity/client's business operation interface arises from the demands made by a project and those made by the ongoing business operation on individual client organisation project contributors. Two separate aspects are worthy of consideration – balancing a staff business role with a staff project role, and the relationship between the project and the host client organisation.

The core business duties of client organisation project contributors may often be inadequately assessed in relation to their required contribution to a project, resulting in underperformance in one or both areas of responsibility and placing individuals in an uncomfortable and indeed unmanageable situation.

On a visitor centre project staff contributors were allocated project roles without further assessment by senior management of the impact of their new role on their existing core business function. While some contributors automatically reprioritised their workload, others tried to maintain their traditional role alongside their project role. Inevitably the pressure of both roles became unmanageable, which caused illness and absence through stress. In addition the project dates were delayed, requiring additional and unbudgeted resources to be brought in at a late stage to address the problems.

A good business relationship between the client organisation and the project cannot be taken for granted. Client organisation personnel may enjoy an unfamiliar degree of autonomy while working on a project and must have clear guidelines to ensure that all efforts are focused on the client organisation's project vision.

On a new visitor centre development, client organisation senior management became increasingly alarmed at the confusion arising from staff project management reports. Neither clear progress nor financial reports were forthcoming. A risk analysis report prepared by consultants identified that the client organisation had not set out clear formal lines of communication and limits of responsibility for staff project contributors. This had led to individual contributors taking project-related decisions without adequate consultation and reference to the client organisation. The project had become increasingly distant and disconnected from the client organisation support mechanisms as a result. Although the actions of individuals were clearly unprofessional, a clearer organisational management process would have controlled the all-too-human failings of personnel.

The National Museums of Scotland began a series of major permanent exhibition gallery developments in 1994. The first stage in the process, led by the then Museums Services Department, was to allocate key management roles to a project director and a design project manager. Clear limits of responsibility were allocated to each. Formal lines of project communication for 'commitment' were then developed and circulated to all team members and to board of management members. The interrelationship and limits of informal communication for 'design development' were also articulated. The result was that from an early stage all team members clearly understood that in a certain context all ideas could be informally and creatively explored, but that committing the organisation to carrying out the ideas required formal approvals and separate formal lines of communication. While it would be incorrect to suggest that no problems arose during the projects, it must be acknowledged that an immediate and responsive communication system had been established between the project team and the client organisation and that the projects were successfully delivered.

HIERARCHY, POWER AND PROFESSIONAL RELATIONSHIPS

Some difficulties will also arise from the more typically observed aspects of group behaviour. Key pragmatic reasons for this will arise from the fact that the group may not have worked together before, or where they have, team members may have differing roles and positions in the new project team. Thus, any team will follow the development stages outlined by Tuckman[2] as 'Forming, Storming, Norming, Performing and Adjourning' (Figure 7.6).

The Tuckman model is a useful tool for understanding generic behavioural characteristics that may be observed during the life of any project. It is also worth noting that there is likely to be iteration between stages of the model and that there are likely to be sub-groups of the project team at differing stages of the model working together simultaneously. There may also be groups who continue to move iteratively between stages, most probably between performing and storming.

Forming	Team members get to know each other, establishing views and goals and behaviour.
Storming	Individuals struggle for position, agree roles and responsibilities and establish communication systems. This stage is often characterised by conflict. Leaders emerge.
Norming	The team achieve and observe a shared set of project values and beliefs and standards of behaviour. A sense of common purpose is achieved.
Performing	The team carry out their individual and collective tasks in the spirit of the new project team.
Adjourning	The project team disband. This stage is unlikely to be simultaneous for all contributors.

Figure 7.6   The Tuckman model

This is partially explained by organisational behaviour but also leads to consideration of the temporary project organisation as a mini 'political system'. The *Concise Oxford English Dictionary*[3] defines politics as 'an organizational process or principle affecting authority, status etc.'. With consideration of politics also comes consideration of power and of influence.

Within the client and design team, a range of views regarding design priorities and issues of importance will exist. This range of views should be used to create a vibrant temporary 'political system' rather than a professional battlefield. A design project requires the coordination of a vast range of criteria and information and to achieve this will require the formation of an appropriate team and project structure comprising a project team hierarchy and lines of communication for formal approval of decisions.

It will be helpful for all contributors if a 'hierarchical map' of project personnel is established at the outset (Figure 7.7). This should recognise the need for informal dialogue within the team in addition to the formal line of communication required to turn an informal discussion into a formal 'project instruction'.

This formally approved personnel map provides in effect a temporary line management structure for the project which establishes the legitimate level of authority and hence power which each team member has in relation to the project. This is useful not only for ensuring that individuals do not exceed their level of authority, but also for ensuring that they meet the minimum level necessary to carry out their role.

Note that more than one map may be needed to distinguish, for example, the 'hierarchy and management structure' from the formal 'lines of communication', illustrating both the formal and informal structures which will coexist. Tables stating key personnel and their roles and responsibilities should supplement the maps where necessary.

FORMATS FOR REPORTING PROGRESS – BALANCING ASPIRATIONS AND MINIMISING CONFLICT

To ensure the correct balance of 'project team/client organisation' and 'client/consultant' aspirations and ideas is maintained, clear communication of a single

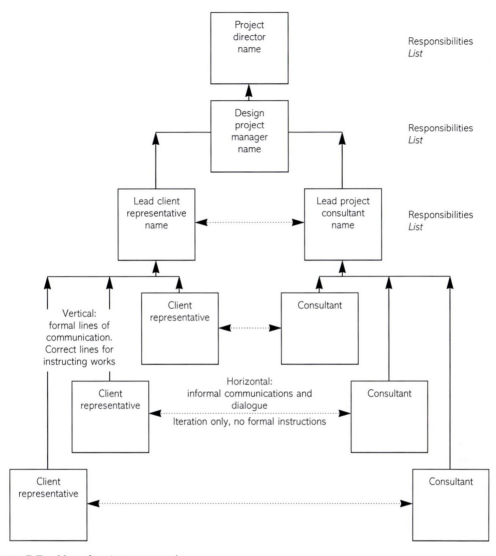

Figure 7.7   Map of project personnel

vision for the project must be ensured. This requires not only strong leadership to identify the vision, but also strong management and administration skills to continuously communicate with the team in the widest sense. Clear project structure and coordinated reporting formats are essential in managing this process.

In addition to explicitly outlining the project structure, the client reporting requirements must therefore be made clear at the outset, including preferred reporting formats and circulation lists for minutes and so on. Besides the many informal meetings which will take place between project contributors, key members of the project team should meet to review progress on a monthly basis during all stages of the project. In the early stages this will help to maintain consistent direction and build momentum, while in the later stages it will be invaluable in supporting decision-taking and identifying how to deal with problems.

Any team structure will generate much verbal and written information. Particularly on large projects, a reporting structure map, similar to the project personnel map in Figure 7.7, should be developed at an early stage. This should consider the main structural issues of information management and reporting requirements. Standard agendas, lists of attendees and frequency of meeting for each reporting group should be agreed at the outset. Dates for meetings may be agreed in advance.

Reporting structure

Figure 7.8 sets out a model structure for coordinating and circulating information on a project-wide basis.

As a further layer of detail, the following provides a structure for the reports required at each level.

Project director's report to board of management
(see also the remarks on the project director's report at the end of Chapter 2)

Purpose: To present the formal 'client organisation's' view of progress on all aspects of the project. Two audiences: formal report to client board of management and shareholders/trustees; also a 'staff update' for all client organisation personnel not involved with the project, and those involved in the project who may not have an overview.

Frequency: Quarterly. Interim reports at key stages if required.

Method of compiling reports: The monthly design project manager's report is the main source of information.

Structure of report: The report may be narrative in form in many aspects, with concise financial and programme reports. It should include overview, key issues, progress achieved, financial assessment. The focus is on what aspects of the 'project vision' have been achieved to date.

Circulation of minutes: May be used not only to communicate key issues relating to progress but also to communicate and reinforce the vision, purpose and significance of the project to the organisation. Speed of issue is not necessarily of the essence, although regularity of issue will command greater respect from all viewers. The report should be issued only after submission to and approval by the client board of management. The design project manager should be in attendance during the project director's presentation of the report to the board of management. Issue to all staff, board of management, trustees, shareholders, design team and contractor contributors – even publish on web site.

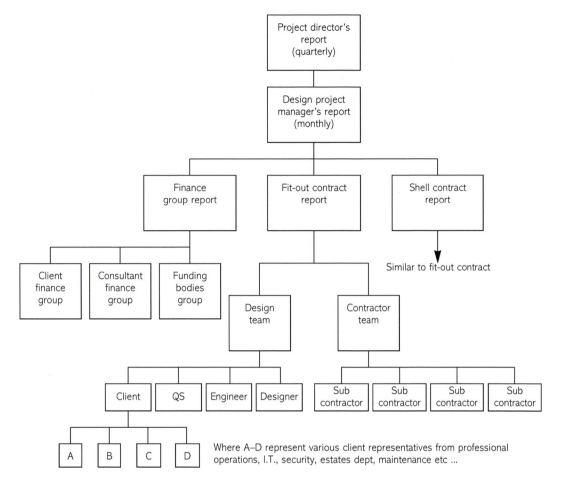

Figure 7.8   Map of reporting structure

Design manager's report to project director

Purpose: To produce a project-wide coordinated view of key aspects of the project that enables confident decision-taking by project contributors and overall direction to be maintained.

Frequency: Monthly.

Method of compiling reports: The project manager should request written reports from each of the key players within the client organisation, design team and perhaps main and specialist contractors and subcontractors, depending on contract strategy. The design project manager should chair a monthly review meeting with these key contributors.

Structure of report: The focus of the report is to summarise key issues from all aspects of the project. It scans the full *breadth* of project concerns. The highest-priority purpose is a review of progress that sets out *future actions required*, rather than an upbeat review of what has taken place. The meeting and subsequent report also permit all contributors to communicate and coordinate future efforts. The written reports from the key contributors noted above should be appended to the report.

Circulation of minutes: To the project director, all key project team members who report directly to the design manager and client organisation board of management. (The board of management will wish to validate and query project director's reports on the basis of the project manager's report.)

The following is a suggested agenda for the monthly design manager's meeting with key project contributors. The first meeting should be used to establish the intention of the monthly meeting forum. The headings given are generic and should be used as a prompt to ensure that appropriate detailed reports are included from individual contributors. A balance should be struck between the desire to include everything and the need to contain the meeting in terms of time. However, a meeting with such a wide remit may be expected to last for half a day.

Chair   Design project manager

Agenda   1. Client contributors' reports
           Shell contract/Estates Dept report
           Fit-out contributors' reports
             Design information
             Operational information issues
             Technical information issues
             Public relations issues
      2. Designers' reports (separate shell and fit-out reports as required)
           Lead consultant
             Fit-out design report
             Shell contract design report
             Interface issues
             Fit-out contract
           Graphic design
           Multimedia
           Lighting
           Mechanical and electrical
      3. Contractors' reports/progress on site
      4. Critical path programme review [design project manager leads this]
      5. Finance report
           Procurement – packages awarded/out to tender/about to go to tender
           Cost report against cost plan

            Contingency report
            Payment
        6. AOB
        7. Next meeting

Individual 'design team' group meetings

Purpose: To coordinate the efforts of various individuals and groups with design and briefing responsibilities.

- Space planning (with sub-groups for various areas)
- Retail
- Catering
- Exhibitions
- Graphics design
- Multimedia design
- Conservation
- Finance
- Programming
- Construction (site meetings, subcontractors' meetings and so on)
- And so on.

Frequency: Weekly or fortnightly formally organised meetings with even more frequent informal meetings. The informal meetings and dialogue between team members reflect the need to explore and develop the qualitative aspects of the design project.

Method of compiling reports: The weekly/fortnightly meeting is an opportunity to assess and record the results of the iterative informal dialogue taking place throughout the week and to adjust if necessary to maintain overall direction and financial/programme control. The formal report records all financial, design, programme and requests for information. Where necessary the design project manager may chair and minute some of the formal meetings.

Circulation: To all immediate team members and to the design project manager.

NOTES

1. Sir J. Egan, *Rethinking Construction*, London: Department of the Environment, Transport and the Regions, 1998.
2. B.W. Tuckman, 'Developmental sequences in small groups', *Psychological Bulletin*, 63 (1965), pp. 384–99.
3. *The Concise Oxford Dictionary*, 9th edn, Oxford University Press, 1996.

8   Tendering and contract strategy for works contractors

PURPOSE

The purpose of this chapter is to provide an introduction to works contract formats, language and processes, and to outline the steps that can be taken by client organisations to assist the management of the works contract strategy and tendering process. It achieves this by presenting basic facts relating to works contracts in a way that assumes no previous knowledge. The emphasis is on providing clarity through an understanding of fundamental principles, using an inclusive approach, rather than giving exhaustive detailed technical information. It is not intended to create contracts managers/administrators but to permit informed client input to the works contract process. Underlying the chapter is the belief that an appropriately structured and coordinated design development process, contract strategy, tendering process and structured tender information are inseparable and must be designed correctly if overall design direction, cost control and progress are to be maintained during the life of the project. This cannot be achieved without an understanding of the contractual process by all contributors.

OUTLINE

- Introduction
- Works contracts overview
- Selecting a contract strategy
- Contract language
- Ensuring an adequate tender package.

INTRODUCTION

When viewing the mountain of works contract documentation that it is possible to generate for a project, it is easy to lose sight of its fundamental purpose. The purpose of a works contract is to provide a formal agreement between a client and a contractor regarding an agreed price and method of payment for an agreed 'scope of works' to be achieved within an agreed timescale, with an agreed methodology, and at an agreed location. The contract also specifies the role of the designer, contract administrator and other consultants within the contract framework, and a mechanism for agreeing costs for variations (additions or omissions) to the tendered works packages by establishing acceptable pre-agreed financial 'rates'.

In an ideal world, decisions regarding all aspects of the design of a project will be taken at an early stage, and the design team will then produce a 'watertight' tender package of drawings and written specifications to which no changes are required to carry out and complete the works. In reality this is rarely achieved. This chapter is therefore about clarity of intent, communication and consistency, emphasising once again the importance of clear information, cooperation and the need for simultaneous informal and formal lines of communication.

WORKS CONTRACTS OVERVIEW

There is a large variety of works contract types, including the Standard Form of Building Contract (SBC), minor works contracts, management contracts, design-and-build contracts and construction management contracts. Although changing legislation means that some aspects of contracts are continually revised, certain fundamentals always apply.

The various forms of contract cater for work packages that differ in terms of their level of expenditure, complexity, and a variety of issues regarding the extent of contractor design services to be procured through the contract. Generally the same project contributors are present in each contract format, but will have differing roles and responsibilities in each; hence it is important to be aware of the general differences in principle. (See also page 100 and Further Information, page 174.)

Parties to the contract

A works contract – like the consultant's contract – is a formal legal agreement between two parties, in this instance the client and the works contractor. There are, however, four parties of major importance involved with a works contract: the employer (client), the contractor, the contract administrator and the quantity surveyor (see Figure 8.1).

The employer

The employer is the term used within the contract for the client organisation who have entered into the contract. Once the contract has 'been let', that is, the contractor has been selected, the formal contractual role of the client is primarily one of ensuring that payments are made. The client cannot issue any instructions to the contractor, and must rely on the contract administrator to do so for the reasons explained later in this chapter. Standard methods and timing for payments to the contractor are determined

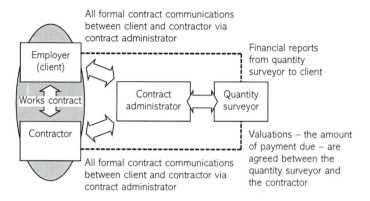

Figure 8.1   Parties to a works contract

within the works contract. Generally, the client makes payment to a contractor on issue of a 'certificate' issued by the contract administrator.

The contractor

The selection of a contractor is usually made via competitive tendering, bringing with it the need for a tender reporting process similar to that outlined earlier in the book for design consultants to facilitate objective decision-making.

There are many types of contractor that a client will hear mentioned during the works stages of the project. Generally, the works contract will involve the client making

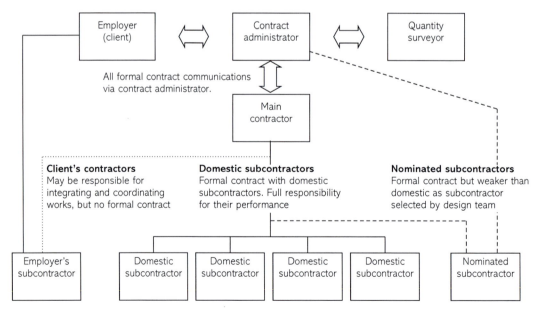

Figure 8.2   Relationship of parties to subcontractors

an agreement with a main contractor. The role of the main contractor is to provide the total scope of works required by the contract and to manage and coordinate all necessary production activity both off and on site.

Where the main contractor cannot tackle certain aspects of the work in house, they will appoint subcontractors. Various contractual relationships exist between a main contractor and their subcontractors depending on the form of contract used and the type of work involved. There is a different contractual relationship between a 'domestic subcontractor', that is, a subcontractor appointed by the main contractor as a part of his tender bid, and a 'nominated subcontractor', that is, a subcontractor appointed by the main contractor at the request of the contract administrator to achieve a particular aspect of the work. The main contractor has full responsibility for ensuring that domestic subcontractors perform to the required standards; this is likely to be more difficult to guarantee with a nominated subcontractor.

There is often a further relationship where a client directly employs a specialist subcontractor to carry out related work without any financial or contractual involvement with the main contractor (see Figure 8.2, on page 122).

The contractor can be expected to provide written reports on the progress of all works packages during the project at site meetings chaired by the contract administrator, and should also hold regular meetings with all subcontractors.

The contract administrator

The role of the contract administrator is to administer the contract impartially on behalf of both the client and the contractor. This is an important role as it forms the interface between 'design intention' and 'financial commitment' on the works contract. The contract administrator is the only project contributor authorised to instruct works, issuing formal 'instructions' that commit the employer financially to each item of work for the contract. The contract administration role in a traditional contract strategy is carried out by the lead designer or architect – hence 'architect's instruction' – however, the role may also be carried by the client, or the main contractor, or by another nominated party, depending on the contract format selected. There is, however, a natural link between the lead designer and the contract administration role.

In addition to committing the employer to financial outlay on the works contract through the issue of 'instructions', the contract administrator, in conjunction with the quantity surveyor, also informs the employer regarding payment due to the contractor by issuing interim or final 'certificates'. The certificates also include 'directions' for the main contractor as to which subcontractors' payments are due within the overall sum. Clients are obliged by the terms of the works contract to make payment to the contractor within 14 days of issue of certificates. The certificates from the contract administrator are in effect to be treated by a client as invoices from the main contractor, although separate VAT invoices or certificates will be required from the contractor for client VAT purposes.

The quantity surveyor

The role of the quantity surveyor includes providing advice regarding project cost planning and works contract strategy options, preparing tender documentation including bills of quantity, tender reports for the contract administrator and regular financial reports for the client. During the works contract, the quantity surveyor will continue to provide contractual advice as required, information that permits the control of costs, and will literally 'value' the works completed on site at regular stages and issue a 'valuation' to the contract administrator. The 'valuation' is a formal contract document that provides the basis for the issue of a corresponding 'interim certificate' by the contract administrator. The contract administrator will most usually follow this valuation advice but has powers to vary it if circumstances dictate. Interim valuations are issued at regular stages during the project on request by the main contractor. A final valuation is issued by the quantity surveyor at the end of the contract upon the making good of all latent defects.

The quantity surveyor may also provide regular cost reports and /or projected cash flow information during the life of the project, depending on the basis of their appointment and the requirements of clients.

The relationships between formally instructing a contractor to proceed with works, the work being carried out, valuation and payment, and the roles of all parties in the process are more readily understood from Figure 8.3. It should also be clear that the process has been designed to explicitly link all parties and ensure that the client only pays an invoice that has been verified by the professional team who will ensure that (a) the correct works have been carried out in accordance with the contract and (b) the cost claimed by the contractor has been correctly valued.

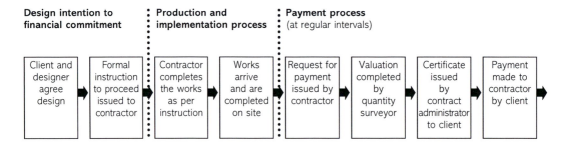

Figure 8.3 Relationships of processes in a contract

SELECTING A CONTRACT STRATEGY

As noted earlier in the chapter, there is a variety of types of works contracts to select from, each with individual characteristics. All forms of contract are in fact variations on the 'traditional' or Standard Form of Building Contract, with more in common than not in terms of process; the main difference is that of repositioned responsibilities and hence roles of the design and construction teams. If the traditional contract roles are understood, the revised roles and actions required should be relatively simple to grasp. The selection of contracts is the subject of many specialist books in its own right; however, the following is a brief overview.

Standard Form of Building Contract (SBC): JCT '80, JCT '98

The text in this chapter thus far is based on the traditional or 'Standard Form of Building Contract' (SBC). This may also be referred to as 'JCT '80' or JCT '98'; both are jargon terms. At the time of writing the latest revision to the SBC was July 2001. The traditional form of contract is structured to permit the appointment of a main contractor to carry out a 'multi-trades' works contract, and all the necessary relationships required to coordinate the design, production and financial activity are defined. The traditional contract route requires that all design and production information be available from the day of appointment of the contractor. Any late design and production information or changes to information may lead to claims for additional payment from the contractor. One major advantage of this form of contract, assuming that the tender information comprises full design production information, and that no changes to the design indicated within the tender documents are made, is that the final cost is known from the outset. If for example all tender costs received were above the cost plan figure, then an informed holistic 'savings' exercise can be carried out with knowledge of the high-cost areas. It is possible to achieve a balanced design/procurement strategy for savings on this basis – preferably as an integral part of the selection and appointment process of the contractor.

The Standard Form of Building Contract (SBC) was used to appoint a main contractor to carry out works to shop-fit a retail bank identity for a major bank within a three-storey listed building. The works involved included the removal of the existing interior, plus making major structural alterations, together with the installation of new electrical and heating services, new internal partitions and specialist screens, new shopfront glazing and a feature clock, some external landscaping and lighting, a new internal public stair, new ceilings, specialist counter design incorporating IT equipment, several ATM cash-in-the-wall machines, bespoke storage and wall lining, bespoke furniture, new floor and wall finishes and so on.

The SBC was appropriate as the architectural practice involved had responsibility for full design and specification of the works, and a full finished set of working drawings – 'production information' – was issued at the tender stage. Completing the works required a number of inputs from specialist subcontractors, many of whom will provide prices to more than one main contractor; one main aspect of bringing the total project together relates to the management skill of the main contractor in co-ordinating the teams of subcontractors involved in addition to the careful selection of suitable subcontractors. The SBC is designed for this type of project.

Minor works contracts are a simple form of contract for works of small financial value, and/or for a single trade contract where no coordination of separate trades is required. (See also Further Information, page 174.)

As a first phase of a major refurbishment project a large public-sector client organisation intended to replace a large area of carpet in their main hall with a new decorative tiled-floor finish. Upon completion of the design and specification scheme a minor works contract tender was issued by the contract administrator to selected flooring contractors. A successful contractor was appointed and a minor works contract signed. Although the flooring design anticipated the future phase two works, no coordination of trades was required as no other trades were involved at this stage. The contract administrator oversaw the contractor on site in conjunction with a client representative. A simple yet appropriate legal, administrative and management system had been utilised.

Management contracts

Management contracts are a variation on the traditional form of contract, where the main contractor provides only management and coordination services direct, with all works packages being provided by separate contracts with subcontractors. Under this form of contract the management contractor may be initially appointed on a tender basis, on a broad scope of works schedule, with an agreed client cost plan, before any design information is available. As this information becomes available, the contractor works closely with the design team to obtain costs from suitable subcontractors through separate tendering processes, reporting and making recommendations on the tenders obtained.

This form of contract is advantageous if aspects of briefing, design and production information will be incomplete at the start of the works, and where a target final cost is to be achieved. The contractor is working as a part of the 'client design team', receiving a fee for the management of the works and a percentage of all instructed works by subcontractors. There is therefore less threat of a 'claims situation' arising.

Some disadvantages with this form of contract do, however, arise. Although the main contractor is less likely to instigate claims for 'late information' in this format, decisions by the design team are being made on the basis of individual works packages on a trickle-feed basis, leaving the potential for later packages to be underfunded if any early cost plan figures are exceeded for any reason.

The developer client of a large commercial waterfront development appointed a management contractor to deliver several key buildings on the basis of the 'building' or 'shell' contract only, that is, no internal fit-out works. Each fit-out contract would be undertaken by a separate main contractor directly employed by the operator of each building. The works involved included all site preparation, drainage works, foundations, steelwork, cladding, several types of specialist roofing, landscaping and so on.

The management contractor collated all production information from the design team involved, issued all tender documents to subcontractors and provided tender reports to the contract administrator and client. All site management and coordination of appointed subcontractors was undertaken by the management contractor.

The contract format was adopted here for several reasons. The project was complex in construction terms relating to groundworks, and in terms of timing related to securing a range of suitable 'operators' and maintaining political approvals. At the point where it was confirmed that works would proceed on site, not all design decisions had been finalised. The contract format permitted production information to be prepared and issued on a controlled staged basis, with a design and construction team in place, when the approval to proceed was given.

With a management contract, as with a traditional contract, the lead designer, contract administrator, quantity surveyor and other consultants remain under the direct appointment of the contract employer (the client). Some of the duties of the quantity surveyor's role under the traditional form of contract are/may be undertaken by the management contractor, for example issue of tenders and tender reporting. Contract administration is not, however, undertaken by the management contractor.

Design-and-build contracts

There are at least two variants of design-and-build contract. Under these forms of contract an employer (client) appoints a main contractor to provide not only works services but also design and all professional services. The advantages to a client probably relate to convenience more than anything else, as the contract structure provides a single point of contact for all aspects of the project.

The differences between the two main variants of design-and-build contracts relate to the method of their initiation. Client organisations may initiate a project as a design-and-build tender by inviting contractors to submit a complete design-and-build tender proposal based on the client design brief. In this instance the proposal will provide not only a cost, but also details of a design team and a design approach all put together by the contractor. The client then has to appraise the design approaches and costs as a package. Advantages of this form of contract are that there is one point of responsibility for a client. Any difficulties with either design or with built quality rest with the contractor's design-and-build team. Disadvantages of this form of contract include a lack of involvement in the design process and a consequent loss of control over costs if changes are required, particularly if requested after appointment of the preferred design-and-build team.

The client may, however, initiate a project by appointing a design team to develop an outline design approach, and subsequently invite contractors to submit a design-and-build proposal for completing the project. The tender invitation may suggest that the contractor completes the design, with the design team remaining employed by the client in an advisory capacity, or may include the requirement for the successful contractor to appoint the client's design team as part of the final design-and-build team in the employment of the contractor. In this instance, since the design team are employed initially by the client and subsequently by the design-and-build contractor, particular care must be taken to ensure that the existing design responsibility is clearly transferred to the design-and-build contractor. The advantages of this form of contract are the same as for the first variant, with the additional advantage that the client has had the benefit of a high degree of control over the initial design approach. Again, however, there may be disadvantages. If a difficulty arises with the design or build quality, the design-and-build contractor may attempt to attribute this to the early stages of design before their involvement, despite the contractual responsibility. In truth, establishing the relationship between design responsibility and build quality can at the best of times be extremely difficult.

With a design-and-build contract, therefore, there may be no direct formal relationship between the client organisation and any of the professional design team, and in that situation all formal communications from the client organisation must be directed via the contractor.

A university developed a design for a refurbished students' union night club with a local architectural/interior design practice. The design proposals were subsequently issued to a number of suitable main contractors as a design-and-build contract tender. Upon receipt and consideration of the design information by the main contractors it became apparent that since such a substantial amount of design work had already taken place, the contract format should be a contractor design portion contract, that is, completion of any incomplete elements of design should only be done by the contractor as the majority of design work was complete. The alternative was for the client to transfer (novate) the responsibility for the existing design to the contractor and for the contractor to subsequently employ the architectural practice.

A privately run sheltered housing operator issued a design-and-build tender to several main contractors with a full list of requirements but no drawings. The proposal was for an extension that was to be fully fitted out and furnished. Each contractor that received the tender had to first employ a design team to begin the process of preparing individual design solutions, costs and methodologies.

Construction management

The final variant of contract outlined here is construction management. This form of contract is broadly similar to a management contract, but here the contractor acts as contract administrator in addition to managing and coordinating subcontractors. In this form of contract the contractor is very much a leading part of the client's professional team, providing advice on design and construction/buildability, tender information issues and cost and programme alongside the design team.

The nature of the forms of contract used for each subcontract package may vary according to their scope of works and may be separate 'contractor design portion' contracts whereby, in addition to construction services, each subcontractor provides design input to complete a scheme design. In this case, the role of the lead designer is to provide design advice regarding the subcontractor's design to the construction manager.

Advantages of this form of contract are similar to those for the management contract route. The construction manager is paid a fee, and the design team and the construction manager work together to ensure that a target budget is achieved. As the construction manager is 'closer' to the design team than in a management contract, further cost and management control may be exercised, particularly on complex projects.

On a new museum project a construction management contract strategy was selected for the fit-out works to address client concerns regarding the slow rate of progress, poor communication by the project team, and the contract management and cost control capabilities of the practice leading the design solution. The construction management team worked with the design practice and client staff representatives to progress and issue tender packages at appropriate stages, and to liaise with package subcontractors to coordinate all design information and activity on site. The client organisation board of management were kept appraised of progress by the construction manager.

CONTRACT LANGUAGE

The following subsections explain common contract-related terms that may be encountered during a project.

Scope of works

The scope of works of the contract is a general description or a list of the works to be carried out under the terms of the contract. It may be organised and/or listed in a variety of ways and levels of detail to aid comprehension, depending on the nature of the project – for example, External Works, Building A, Building B. An executive summary of the works involved.

Bill of quantities

The bill of quantities, prepared by a quantity surveyor, is used to obtain competitive tender costs from a variety of contractors and to agree rates for variations and final account costs with the successful contractor. It starts with the scope of works and provides as much itemised detail as the 'production information' (see below) produced by the design team permits. The bill of quantities forms one part of the contract documentation.

Production information

Production information is the term used to describe the working drawing and written specification information prepared by the design team. It permits the production/manufacture of a design to be carried out by a contractor or subcontractor. Production information is used initially to prepare a bill of quantities and obtain competitive tenders.

Cost plan

A cost plan relates to the scope of works of a contract and the total budget approved by a client organisation. Target budgets are allocated to each major element within the scope of works, and these cost plan figures are subsequently used to make informed decisions as tenders are received. Where tenders received are greater than the cost plan figure a 'savings' exercise is required.

Cost reports

Cost reports relate to financial progress made relative to the cost plan. Regular cost reports should be provided to a client during the project and should be formatted simply to permit direct reference to the cost plan headings. Further detail on, say, the use of contingencies and forecasts of final out-turn should be given within the cost reports.

Architect's instruction

(Contract administrator's instruction/construction manager's instruction and so on)

The 'instruction' system is the only formal means of passing requests for work to a contractor. Only the contract administrator may issue an instruction. This ensures that the contractor does not implement informal verbal requests. The employer (client) cannot instruct the contractor to carry out work under the terms of the contract other than via the contract administrator. An architect's/contract administrator's/ construction manager's/instruction is the formal 'confirmation to proceed' given to a contractor. This formally commits the client financially to an item of work under the terms of the contract.

Variation

A variation is any change to an item of work from that described in the original tender documents. Any variation to a contract must be formally confirmed by the contract administrator on an 'instruction'. This ensures that there is a record of the variations required from the contractor and a mechanism for recording the change in cost. A variation may be an addition or a reduction in works/cost. The reasons for variations should be noted at the time of instruction.

Snagging

Snagging is the process of inspecting works carried out by the contractor for incomplete or poor workmanship. It is usually done before practical completion (see below) is achieved, and must be rectified before a Certificate of Practical Completion (see below) is issued.

Practical completion

In order that a contractor may coordinate all activity and health and safety on a site, the client must hand over control of that site to the contractor on commencement of the works, and the contractor thereafter controls access of all personnel to the site. This includes access to the site by the client. The contractor is also responsible for insurance of the building/area of the works for the duration of the works contract. Practical completion is the formal stage of a works contract at which responsibility for control of access and for insurance and health and safety passes back to the client/employer.

Practical completion is issued to a contractor when the works are completed to such an extent that will permit a client to use the works. A Certificate of Practical Completion is issued by the contract administrator when the design team is satisfied that all works as described in the contract documents, including all instructed variations, have been carried out. The Certificate of Practical Completion is an important document as it:

- permits release of half the contract retention sum to the contractor, usually one half of 3 per cent;
- releases the contractor from his liability to pay L&A (liquidate and ascertained) damages (see below);
- starts the defects liability period.

Practical completion should be issued at a formal handover meeting on site with the contractor, contract administrator, designer and the client/employer. Where relevant, all keys and maintenance manuals/health and safety file should be handed over to the client by the contractor. All contractor's property should have been removed from the site by this stage unless a partial possession is being agreed. The assembled parties should walk around all areas of the works and any defects observed should be noted and excluded from the Certificate of Practical Completion if necessary.

Beneficial or partial occupation

Where a client seeks to have access to a building or interior before the issue of practical completion, for example where a contract date for completion has not been met, a 'beneficial' or 'partial occupation' arrangement must be agreed with the contractor. This may be along the lines of agreeing a date for occupation but withholding release of the retention sum and postponing the start date for latent defects liability, but releasing the contractor from the need to pay L&A damages. Responsibility for insurances should be transferred to the employer. A revised form of the Certificate of Practical Completion may be used to achieve this. The contract administrator should not be pressured into issuing practical completion.

Payment

The following items relate to documentation and procedures for methods of payment in a works contract.

Interim valuations and final valuation

Valuations are issued to the contract administrator by the quantity surveyor. Without a valuation, it is not possible for the contract administrator to issue a certificate, or for a client to make payment to a contractor. Interim valuations are issued at regular intervals during the works, usually every four weeks. A final valuation is issued upon the issue of a 'certificate of completion of making good defects' at the end of the latent defects period.

Interim certificates and Final Certificate

Certificates are issued by the contract administrator. They correspond to and verify the valuations issued by the quantity surveyor and are treated by the client in effect as an invoice from the contractor. Interim certificates correspond to interim valuations, and the Final Certificate corresponds to the Final Valuation. The Final Certificate is the final payment to the contractor of the remaining retention sum, usually one half of 3 per cent. Issue of the Final Certificate signifies the end of the contract.

Retention

The contract retention sum is a percentage of the contract value, usually 3 per cent, which is withheld in full from payments to the contractor on each interim valuation and certificate until issue of the Certificate of Practical Completion. When practical completion is achieved, one half of the retention is released. The final retention is released when the contractor has rectified all latent defects and the contract administrator issues the Final Certificate. The intention of the retention system is to provide an added stimulus to the contractor to achieve first practical completion, and finally make good all latent defects noted by the client, designer and contract administrator at the end of the latent defects period.

Extension of time

An extension of time is awarded to a contractor when events outwith their control affect the progress of the works. When an extension of time is awarded by the contract administrator, the contractor is due corresponding additional preliminaries or site establishment costs. No liquidate and ascertained (L&A) damages (see below) are payable to the client for an extension of time.

Liquidate and ascertained (L&A) damages

Liquidate and ascertained damages are often confused with the so-called 'penalty clause'. The term refers to a sum of money per week/month which is incorporated into a contract to compensate a client organisation for any financial losses which it will incur, for example loss of trading and so on, if contract completion dates are not met by the contractor. The extent of the client's loss must be substantiated, and it is easier to prove a loss of trading and so on for an established business than to prove any losses for a new venture or a not-for-profit entity. However, if L&A damages are built into a contract, at a rate of say £1000 per week, and delays occur for which no extension of time is due, then provision is made for negotiation. The L&A damages clause is not an opportunity for a client organisation to profit from a late-running contract!

Latent defects period, latent defect and making good of latent defects

Works contracts have a 'latent defects period' of six or twelve months. A latent defect is an item of work carried out by the contractor which is not in accordance with the contract specification and which might not be apparent at practical completion/ handover, but which becomes apparent in use during the latent defects period. The latent defects period starts at practical completion and runs for the period specified within the contract. At the end of the latent defects period the client, designer and contract administrator inspect the works and issue a schedule of latent defects to the contractor. The contractor makes good these defects, at no cost to the client, and the contract administrator issues a 'certificate of completion of making good defects'.

This certificate permits a Final Valuation and then Final Certificate to be issued, and final release of retentions to be made. The client makes the final payment to the contractor and the obligations of all parties under the contract are ended.

CDM regulations

The Construction Design and Management (CDM) regulations are intended to integrate health and safety into the design and construction process so that all parties – client, designer and contractors – have an interlinked responsibility for safe design and construction. Some of the key aspects of CDM relate to the need for a client to appoint a planning supervisor, the preparation of a pre-tender health and safety plan by the planning supervisor, and the preparation at practical completion stage of a health and safety file. The health and safety file, containing as-built drawings and manuals, suppliers, method statements and so on, is in effect a 'user's manual' and is handed over to the client at practical completion. It is intended to permit safe maintenance of the works and even safe dismantling/removal or redesign of the works by an unknown future design team.

Planning and building regulations

Before proceeding with work on any project the necessary planning permissions, notices or consents must be obtained. This is also essential if changes to listed buildings are intended. It is particularly important to ensure that planning permission will be granted before embarking on a large volume of design work, and informal discussion with the planning department at an early stage will provide an indication of their likely response to a proposal. Local authority and building regulations, which, for example, differ in Scotland and England, must be checked to ensure that all building works will comply. No physical works should be undertaken without first making the appropriate application. The responsibility for ensuring that all works comply with the building regulations usually rests with the lead design consultant.

Planning permission is controlled by the local authority planning department, which ensures that all building works are appropriately designed for the area in which the works are proposed by issuing planning permission for a project upon receipt and approval of satisfactory design drawings and written specifications. Their particular concerns include aesthetics and materials proposed, but also proposed business use and access, parking provision and so on. No works should be carried out without planning permission. Obtaining planning permission is generally the responsibility of the lead design consultant. Details of how to proceed can be obtained from the local council and can often be found on their website.

ENSURING AN ADEQUATE TENDER PACKAGE

Avoiding ambiguity

Since the degree of financial and programme control is influenced by the degree to which the tender information completely describes the design intention, it is important to ensure that the production information which is prepared for the tender package is as complete as possible. The client/consultant briefing interface is an important area to consider again as it must be managed effectively during the tender package preparation stages to clarify where responsibility lies.

During the process of developing a tender package for a project, clients should permit the consultants involved to exercise the full scope of their professional services in preparing the information. This is to ensure that no constraints are placed on their capacity to produce comprehensive tender information. This in turn means that the consultants have responsibility for ensuring that the tender information is completed to an extent that fully describes the design in all required detail, leaving no scope for additional work by the contractor and subsequent unforeseen costs arising.

To avoid ambiguity regarding responsibility for the degree of completeness of the tender information, the client must have provided all necessary briefing information. If the briefing has been completed, the design team should be in a position to prepare a comprehensively detailed and specified tender package, requiring little or no additional design information. There is therefore little, or no, scope for any change in cost or timescale.

With a view to ensuring that the brief doesn't change at this late stage, it is also important to consider again the interface between a project and the client organisation. The organisation must be fully aware of, and supportive of, all design and procurement decisions that have been taken before preparing tender information. Any conflict between the project and the client organisation that has not been resolved by tender stage will introduce risk to financial and programme control through the need for changes to the scope of works post tender stage. The required reporting methodologies led by the design project manager are discussed in Chapter 7.

> During the preparation of tender documents for a natural heritage visitor attraction, several audiovisual programmes had been specified. Following acceptance of the successful contractors and at a relatively late stage of the development of the audiovisual programmes, it became apparent that the necessary services infrastructure required to control the films, and other multimedia, was based on an out-of-date method of client operation. The client brief given at the time of tender document preparation was for individually controlled units that would be controlled by a member of staff – as was the case at other existing but smaller facilities. The new brief specified a centralised control point for all multimedia, audiovisual and lighting and so on, requiring a revised audiovisual hardware specification and cost in addition to changes to the newly completed building works with further associated costs.

Reporting

The previous subsection has made it clear that clear and effective communication is essential during these stages. To ensure an adequate tender package is prepared, the following gives guidelines for reporting.

Design development reports

Since the tender production information arises from the expression in technical terms of the design intention, the client organisation must fully support all such decisions taken. This must be fully resolved before preparation of the tender information to remove any risk that change will be required. This process, led by the design project manager, is considered in more detail in terms of structure and reporting formats in Chapter 7.

Works contractors' shortlist report

The client organisation should be given the opportunity to influence the shortlist of works contractors. Depending on the scale of the project this may be a simple verbal report or a written report, and interview with contractors. An explicit attempt should be made to obtain information, good and/or bad, from other clients regarding any previous experience with contractors. The purpose of the report is to obtain approval of the client organisation, a mechanism that also engages them with the project decision-making process. The design project manager will be responsible for managing the involvement of the client organisation as outlined in Chapter 7.

Works contract strategy report

During the design development and production information process, the design team should be formulating a suitable supporting contract strategy. When a decision has been agreed, this must be reported to the client organisation, with option appraisal information stating the reasons for the strategy selected. The purpose of the report is to permit comment from the client organisation, a mechanism that also engages them with the project decision-making process.

Pre-tender probable cost report

When a tender package is issued, the design team should already have reported to the client organisation with a reasonable degree of certainty, the anticipated financial outcome of the tender process. A meaningful pre-tender 'probable cost' document requires comprehensive production information (working drawings and specification) based on an accurate brief. The report should outline a strategy for dealing with any financial difficulties that are forecast, and will be submitted initially to the design project manager for circulation within the client organisation.

Tender report

The lead party responsible for issuing a tender report will vary depending on the contract strategy. However, the design project manager/director should provide an overall report for a client's board of management which interprets the information produced by the professional design team and provides clear recommendations for action. The format of the tender report will depend very much on the scope of the works involved, but like any report must be hierarchically structured in order that an overview of the situation proceeds the detail. Qualitative issues must be considered in addition to cost.

Monthly design project managers' reports

The monthly meetings and reports/minutes prepared by the design project manager and described in Chapter 7 of this book, will assist in the timely circulation of, and response to, all of the above reports on a integrated and project wide basis.

9 Project management

PURPOSE

Underlying the philosophy of this book is the belief that the business of a client organisation, the briefing for a design project, the conceptual design process and the remaining design and production processes cannot be regarded as separate, unrelated entities. The purpose of this chapter, then, is to provide client organisations with an overall outline of the entire design project management process from inception to post completion. It summarises what has been explained in more detail in earlier chapters, providing an overview of the overall project process context, and therefore draws the many aspects of the book together. It approaches the overview in a manner that 'freezes' and articulates the key stages within what is actually a fluid and seamless process. It achieves this by outlining the project process using the stages and terminology developed over many years by the Royal Institute of British Architects, but with interpretation and language from a client's, rather than a designer's perspective. The RIBA Plan of Work was originally published in 1964 to provide a model procedure for design team working and was produced in response to industry reports of the time noting the need for improved communications within the construction industry. It was substantially updated in 1998 to reflect changes in design and procurement practice, legislation and contemporary industry reports.[1]

The emphasis given in the Plan of Work is to some extent reversed in this book by interpreting the process model in a manner more appropriate to a client's rather than a designer's perspective within the process. By becoming familiar with the Plan of Work, client representatives gain substantially from the improved communication made possible through knowledge of the language, terminology and methodologies used by design and construction professionals. Without this understanding, a barrier is effectively created which will create 'distancing' between the project's key players – the client and the lead designer.

The original Plan of Work was written with the stated assumption that 'the architect is responsible for leading the client and the design team'. This situation is no longer automatically true, as reflected in the 1998 edition of the Plan of Work which contains alternative plan of work models for two design-and-build routes of procurement.

Interestingly, some of the changes in the revised 1998 Plan of Work reflect a move towards integrating the client's involvement into the process. They include a brief note about 'establishing the need' before the Plan of Work process, a simplification of the plan of work model into three phases instead of four, plus models for the design-and-build procurement methods often favoured by client organisations.

OUTLINE

- Introduction
- Stages of a project RIBA Plan of Work
- Progress reporting formats
- Financial reporting formats
- Change control mechanisms
- Liaison and coordination with parallel buildings contracts.

INTRODUCTION

A key aspect of this chapter is the overview of the architect's Plan of Work interpreted from a client's perspective. In fact, the Plan of Work and this book have much in common. Both start with the recognition that while all projects are made up of very different variables, there are none the less inevitably more similarities than differences in the processes of each project. It is also interesting to note that the Plan of Work definition of the lead designer's role is split into two distinct but interwoven components – architect as lead consultant (previously 'management function') and architect as designer/design leader (previously 'design function'). The lead consultant role as defined within the Plan of Work, with its close relationship to the 'designer/design leader' role, reflects several aspects of the client design management role outlined within this book.

The main difference between the Plan of Work and this book is the range of issues considered, and the perspective taken on that range of issues. The book synthesises business concern with design concern, and views the process and the criteria for success from the client's rather than the designer's perspective.

STAGES OF A PROJECT RIBA PLAN OF WORK

The architect's Plan of Work splits the entire project process into three main phases:

1 Feasibility
2 Pre-construction
3 Construction.

Within each of these key phases, there are identifiable stages from A to L, each of which it is important to understand, as they may be linked to design practice appointment contracts and fee payments.

Client design brief issued to shortlisted design practices/teams

Appointment of design consultants following appraisal and interview

No changes to brief beyond this point

Changes to the design beyond this point will incur additional fees and other costs resulting from abortive work and/or work additional to the agreed resource plan

Phase 1 Feasibility		Phase 2 Pre-construction period						Phase 3 Construction period		
Appraisal	Strategic briefing	Outline proposals	Detailed proposals	Final proposals	Production information	Tender documentation	Tender action	Mobilisation	Construction to practical completion	After practical completion
Stage A	Stage B	Stage C	Stage D	Stage E	Stage F	Stage G	Stage H	Stage J	Stage K	Stage L
Discrete mini-project completed and led by client		Creative tender process	Main iterative stages							
Client organisation lead		Design team lead						Client leads		

Figure 9.1 Plan of work for a traditional contract strategy
Source: RIBA © RIBA Publications

The Plan of Work for a traditional contract strategy may be set out as in Figure 9.1.

In reality, of course, it is rare to find a project that proceeds in quite such a mechanistic and linear fashion. However, it is important to understand the theoretical model so that the implications of any variations from it may also be understood, not only by individual contributors, but also by the team collectively. Variations from the linear model may occur at any stage of the project; for example, for reasons arising from changes to client input/resources, or from contract strategy selection, or from problems arising on site during construction. This book considers that Phase 1, 'Feasibility', should be carried out as a discrete mini-project in its own right so that a competitive concept tender process may be carried out during Stage C of the Plan of Work. The intention is to permit clients to obtain a range of conceptual design approaches before appointing a lead design consultant, at the end of Stage C, to develop the concept design towards completion.

The Plan of Work provides a double-page layout for each stage that sets out a matrix of the key actions and responsibilities for each team member. It correlates simultaneous and sequential actions and responsibilities for:

- The client
- The architect as lead consultant (could also be client design project manager)
- The architect as designer and design leader (could be another design discipline)
- Quantity surveyor
- Structural engineer
- Services engineer
- Planning supervisor
- Contractor (Stages J, K and L only).

Each stage is interpreted for client organisations within this chapter.

Phase 1 – Feasibility

The feasibility phase comprises two RIBA Plan of Work stages, Stage A 'Appraisal' and Stage B 'Strategic briefing'. Both are detailed more fully in Chapters 2, 3 and 4 but are outlined here as an integral part of the overview of all the Plan of Work stages. The feasibility phase may be completed by in-house staff where the client organisation has appropriately experienced design project management staff, and regularly carries out 'capital works' projects as part of its overall operation – for example, retail operators, restaurant operators, leisure operators, banks/building societies, museums and so on. However, for many client organisations, particularly those faced with a one-off project, much benefit will be gained from the external professional advice of a design manager.

Stage A – Appraisal

At the appraisal stage, the client will still be determining what business objectives are to be achieved from a design project, and what resources are to be made available.

Appraisal is the stage at which the client puts together an internal organisation to support the project, including the appointment of a project director, design project manager and all other advisers. In addition to establishing the internal team, this stage also includes identifying the future need for input from other consultants. The task is to complete an outline of the project that is acceptable to a client organisation board of management that may be further developed during the feasibility phase. This will include outline thoughts on budget, timescale and business gain/level of creativity aspired to.

Stage B – Strategic briefing

Before embarking on preparation and consideration of outline proposals by design practices/team, the client organisation should investigate broad parameters of the project to determine whether the objectives identified at inception are achievable in an acceptable manner. There are several aspects to consider:

- Functional feasibility – in terms of client operational requirements, physical requirements, site conditions and so on
- Technical feasibility – in terms of statutory consents, physical requirements, time constraints and the like
- Financial feasibility – capital costs, revenue costs, maintenance issues and cash flow/financial year constraints
- Business feasibility – does the strategic briefing analysis indicate that the qualitative aspects of the project correctly 'match' or 'fit' with the business model of the client organisation?
- Strategic fit
- Marketing fit
- Operational fit.

To achieve the successful outcome of this stage requires the study of client operational requirements, including identification and coordination of all client department interface parameters, at least in principle, that is, security, shopfloor operation, as well as site-specific and cost programme parameters.

The advice of the design project manager during these stages will be invaluable in objectively progressing matters.

Phase 2 – Pre-construction

The pre-construction phase comprises six RIBA Plan of Work stages:

- Stage C 'Outline proposals'
- Stage D 'Detailed proposals
- Stage E 'Final proposals'
- Stage F 'Production information' (two sub-stages here)

- Stage G 'Tender documentation'
- Stage H 'Tender action'.

The work stages of this phase are concerned with producing, in the first instance, tangible evidence of the brief; developing a concept design in an iterative and consultative manner, from initial descriptive information to full technical drawing information that will permit competitive-market-tested costs to be obtained from a tender process. More than any other, this phase represents the interface between briefing and design.

Stage C – Outline proposals

The purpose of the outline proposal stage is to provide the client with the first tangible evidence of the potential range of design opportunities that might arise from design analysis of the client design brief. This will include options regarding general arrangement, form, layout, materials and construction. In terms of the design management philosophy of this book, Stage C represents the stage at which client organisations issue the client design brief/tender invitations seeking conceptual design approaches from design practices/teams.

If this process is followed, at the end of this stage, client organisations will have analysed a range of conceptual design and construction approaches to the client design brief via the tender process.

The analysis involved during this stage will include consideration of a variety of general arrangement design studies, noting the disadvantages, advantages and opportunities presented by each option/approach. The aim is to seek and gain executive board of management approval for the preferred route forward from the client organisation, regarding the match of the preferred general design principles meeting the already established business brief. This will include initial cost, procurement and programme data and analysis specific to each design proposal.

This stage as outlined in this book ends with the appointment of the successful design practice/team. More detail is given in Chapters 4, 5 and 6.

Stage D – Detailed proposals

Within the guidelines put forward by this book Stage D is the first point at which the client is working with their fully appointed design team. Upon completion of Stage C and appointment of a design practice/team, the purpose of Stage D is to conclude the project team design brief and to establish a detailed design package that articulates all aspects of the design. It achieves this by providing a tangible framework of drawings and models and so on within which the detailed design can be seen to respond fully to the client design brief in terms of aesthetics, plan arrangement, accommodation, materials and finishes vocabulary, construction methodology, programme and cost build-up.

The client must understand their part in this process, particularly during this important, almost final, part of the 'brief to design' synthesis. The client should also understand the part played by the design team, particularly the lead design consultant, in the process. By this point, a total match of 'aspirations to expectations' must exist to permit a meaningful financial assessment to be made. The lead design consultant, working alongside the design manager, plays the major part in ensuring that a full schedule of information required to complete the design is prepared, enabling an appropriate cost plan figure to be provided by the supporting design team quantity surveyor.

The project team design must be frozen by completion of this stage to ensure control over the design and any subsequent impact on programme and costs, including professional fees. Planning consent would normally be applied for during this stage.

Stage E – Final proposals

The purpose of Stage E is to achieve final agreement between the client organisation and design practice/team on all matters relating to the design. During this stage, the design information must be developed to a point that permits the subsequent coordinated preparation of all technical drawings and specifications by all team members. The information produced by the design team must articulate:

- All elements of the design
  - Final general arrangement drawings, plans, sections, elevations, sketches as required
  - Final schedules of accommodation/requirement for all elements of the design
  - Final services information
  - Final materials specifications and outline construction specifications
  - Final performance specifications for all elements
- Construction methodologies and procurement strategy
- Cost (pre-tender 'budget elemental cost' prepared by the design team quantity surveyor)
- Programme.

This can only be achieved if the client organisation and design team have collectively identified and articulated all items required. This means that the client organisation ensure that during Stage D and the early part of Stage E, all the requirements of the client design brief are satisfied by the design.

Exact headings for inclusion will depend on the nature of the project and the 'method of measurement' adopted by the quantity surveyor, but typically, the information will include the items shown in Figure 9.2.

Stage E is the final iterative design stage. Beyond this stage, the process moves towards a linear technical design development process driven by the design team, coordinated and led by the lead design consultant. Stage E is the final stage at which any changes to the design, which even then must be minor, may be contemplated without resulting in abortive work and consequent additional costs.

- Survey drawings/information of all existing elements
- Downtakings
- Substructure
- Groundworks
- Primary elements
  - New structural walls
  - Floors
  - Roofs
  - Stairs ramps and so on
  - Internal structural alterations
- Secondary elements
  - Windows
  - External doors
  - Internal doors
  - Ceilings
  - Roof lights
  - Internal partitions
  - Fireplaces
  - Special features
- Finishes
  - Walls
  - Floors
  - Ceilings
  - Special features/fitments
- Services and installations
  - Drainage
  - Water supply
  - Electrical
  - Gas
  - Heating
  - Mechanical air handling/conditioning
  - IT
  - Telecoms/communications
  - Lighting
  - Security
  - Fire
  - Refuse
- Fixtures
  - Reception
  - Circulation area
  - Public areas
  - Offices
  - Exhibition areas
  - Dining
  - Bedrooms
  - Seating
  - Kitchens
  - Bathrooms
  - Lavatories
  - Cleaning
  - Storage
- Furnishings
  - Carpets/rugs
  - Curtains/blinds/shutters
  - Screens
  - Ornaments
  - Art: paintings, sculpture and so on
  - Seating
  - Tables
  - Desks
  - Storage
  - Interior planting
- Specialist works
  - Multimedia
  - Audiovisual
  - Lifts

Sources: Combination of sources, including D. Dry, *The Interior Design Workbook*, London: Architecture and Building Practice Design Guides Ltd, 1983

Figure 9.2   Stage E checklist

Stage F – Production information

The purpose of Stage F is to develop the Stage E information into the working drawings, specifications and schedules required to prepare the works tender information and related contract documentation (that is, the 'production or manufacturing information') and to obtain any final statutory consents such as building control. It is a technical design process. The Stage F information will provide the basis of the contractual agreement with a main contractor and all subcontractors involved, and should include all the information they will each require to manufacture, deliver, install and hand over the finished works to the client.

Stage G – Tender documentation

Stage G is to some degree a continuation of Stage F. However, it is a stage that is usually led by the quantity surveyor using the production information produced by the design team during Stage F to produce a bill of quantities. The purpose of the bill of quantities is to supplement the production information by itemising and scheduling all the elements of the design required to complete the works. This includes not only the items indicated on the drawings and specifications, but also other conditions that are required to carry out the works. This includes site access, and site establishment plus management and contract conditions that are specific to the project.

The headings in a bill of quantities will vary depending on the contract format, but will typically be as shown in Figure 9.3.

- Preliminaries/general conditions
- Client organisation and design team contacts
- Tender and contract documents schedule
- The site, site access and site facilities required, and any conditions applying to the successful contractor, security, travel, protection and so on
- Description of the works
- Items for fixed and time related costs (plant, temporary works)
- Contract: form of contract, variations to standard clauses, supplementary clauses, conditions, definitions and so on
- Pre-contract health and safety plan
- The works bill and specifications
- Headings will depend on the nature of the project. Individual bills will be listed by trade much as itemised earlier in Stage E (see Figure 9.2)
- Qualifications and amplifications
- Provisional sums
- Dayworks
- General summary and collection of costs listed by trade

Figure 9.3   Headings in a bill of quantities

Some issues for a client to consider during this stage include ensuring that any organisational procedures, whether policy or operational, are incorporated into the tender process, for example:

- The number of contractors that must be issued with a tender enquiry
- All contractors signing a *bona fide* tender certificate
- Provision of unmarked tender envelopes
- Procedures for receiving, opening and recording tenders
- Security procedures
- Site-specific operational issues.

During this stage, at the latest, suitable contractors for the work should be identified. This is more difficult than it appears at first sight. Turnover of contractor personnel and variations in workload are two issues vital to ensuring quality of work, and it is obvious that shortlisting a contractor on the basis of one project is no guarantee of the same service and standard of work on the next. Another issue, driven by commercial rather than human considerations, is the attitude taken by the contractor to contract claims. The views of the contract administrator and the quantity surveyor regarding recent performance of suitable contractors will be invaluable here. In some business sectors, however, client organisations themselves will have greater knowledge of the overall performance of contractors than their consultants, so it is important that the experience of the entire project team is shared and utilised.

For all the reasons noted, and for other reasons that will undoubtedly arise from project-specific criteria, it is advisable to meet with a range of contractors to identify their level of interest in carrying out a project. The meeting will also serve as an opportunity to seek assurances with regard to current workload, resources, personnel and recent clients and to query these in relation to project-specific issues before creating a shortlist.

Stage H – Tender action

The purpose of Stage H is to gain a range of current, 'market-tested' costs for the works from a range of selected contractors. During much of the production information, tender documentation and tender action stages, client representatives are likely to have a secondary rather than a lead role. The design team should be permitted to exercise their professional responsibilities to the full so that responsibility for the completeness of the tender package is clearly defined. The key issue for the client has been to ensure that the brief completely meets all their business requirements, and that the design fully satisfies the brief.

Phase 3 – Construction

The construction phase comprises three RIBA Plan of Work stages:

- Stage J 'Mobilisation'
- Stage K 'Construction to practical completion'
- Stage L 'After practical completion'.

At this stage the project process, already technical and linear, becomes even more formal and linear, particularly so with traditional works contract format. This is largely due to the nature of contract administration that demands formal communication procedures to ensure control. During these stages client organisations that are unfamiliar with project work may begin to feel peripheral to some degree, as the majority of dialogue will be between the design team and the contractor.

Stage J – Mobilisation

Stage J involves appointing the successful main contractor, the formal issue of all production information via formal contract 'Instruction', plus agreeing the main contractor's programme and methodology for achieving the works. The contract administrator leads this stage.

The contract administrator chairs two important meetings during this stage. The first is the erroneously titled 'pre-contract' meeting at which all information is issued to the contractor, and all project objectives, roles and responsibilities of all team members, and project methodologies including lines of communication are set out.

Agenda: Pre-contract meeting	
	Action
Introductions	
Appointments, personnel	
Roles and responsibilities	
Project description	
Contract	
Priorities	
Handover of production information	
Commencement and completion dates	
Insurances	
Bond (if applicable)	
Standards and quality	
Contractors matters	
Possession	
Programme	
Health and safety file and plan	
Site organisation, facilities and planning	
Security	
Site restrictions	
Contractor's quality control policy and procedures	
Statutory undertakers	
Overhead and underground services	
Temporary services	
Signboards	
Clerk of works matters	
Roles and duties	
Facilities	
Liaison	
Dayworks	
Consultants matters	
Lead design consultant	
Structural engineer	
Mechanical	
Electrical	
Others	
Quantity surveyor's matters	
Adjustments to tender figures	
Valuation procedures	
Remeasurement	
VAT	
Communications and procedures	
Information requirements	
Distribution of information	
Valid instructions	
Lines of communication	
Dealing with queries	
Building control notices	
Meetings	
Pattern and proceedings	
Status of minutes	
Distribution of minutes	
Circulation: Contractor, client organisation design team	

Source: S. Cox et al., *The Architect's Job Book*, 6th edn, London: RIBA Publications © RIBA Publications

Figure 9.4   Agenda for a pre-contract meeting

Immediate actions are established for the contractor and the design team. It is an opportunity to introduce and build the new wider project team. The agenda should be developed from the checklist of potential contributors' reports given in Figure 9.4.

Just as the lead design consultant and other design team contributors must brief the contractor on the particular detail of the works, the client should brief the contractor on any operational business issues that must be taken into account during the construction period. The intention is to enable the contractor to prepare appropriately detailed proposals which are responsive to the carrying out of all aspects of the specific project works.

Much of this meeting will reiterate the details of the contract tender package to a large extent, but this serves to ensure that all parties have clearly understood the contractual obligations before formal commitment to proceed. This will include discussion of the client's obligation to hand over control of the building or site to the contractor, and ensuring that the contractor has all necessary insurances in place. If any variation has taken place from the tender documentation dates for commencement of the works, this should be formally recorded, as the completion date must also change accordingly.

The contractor 'takes possession' of the site to ensure the management and control of personnel and plant on site. This aspect may seem odd to some clients initially, but it is an essential and inevitable aspect of this stage. In theory a contractor can refuse anyone access to the site. This necessity for a contractor to control access to the site of the works means that where there is a physical interface between a client's business operation and the project works, a set of agreed detailed procedures for managing the two parallel sets of activities must be established.

The second meeting the contract administrator will chair is a follow-on pre-site start meeting at which the main contractor's proposals and final arrangements for site operations are reviewed, adjusted as necessary and finally agreed. The agenda for a pre-start meeting using the minutes generated by the pre-contract meeting might be as shown in Figure 9.5.

The client's interests should be fully represented at all stages of the mobilisation and construction period, via the attendance of their design project manager and appropriate staff representatives.

Agenda: Pre-start site meeting

Confirmation of outstanding items from pre-contract meeting

Settlement of queries

Examination of contractor's programme including key dates for the supply of any outstanding information

Agree methods of progressing

Circulation: Contractor, client organisation, design team

Source: RIBA Plan of Work, original version © RIBA Publications

Figure 9.5   Agenda for a pre-start site meeting

The lead design consultant, whether contract administrator or not, remains responsible for coordinating technical design input from other design disciplines during this and subsequent stages.

Stage K – Construction to practical completion

Stage K is the period in which all physical works take place. It begins with the contractor 'taking possession' of the site at Stage J, and ends with 'practical completion' – the handover of the finished project back to the client.

During this stage, depending on the contract strategy and consultant appointments, the contract administrator or lead design consultant will chair regular site meetings at weekly or fortnightly intervals at which the client organisation must be represented. A typical agenda is given in Figure 9.6.

Ideally, during this stage, no new production information will be required to complete the design and no changes will be made. This will provide maximum control over costs and programme. It is important for clients to be aware that only the contract administrator may formally issue 'instructions' to the contractor to formally vary the

---

Agenda: Site meetings

	Action
Minutes of last meeting and actions arising	
Contractor's report	
Overview report (narrative)	
Subcontractor's report	
Progress	
Programme	
Health and safety report	
Information received since last meeting	
Information required	
Instructions required	
Design project manager's report	
Lead design consultant's report	
Structural engineer's report	
Mechanical and electrical engineers' reports	
Quantity surveyor's report	
Client's report	
All client contributors	
AOB	
Communications and procedures	
Contract completion date review, delays?	
Separate meetings to review information? Costs? Programme?	
Next meeting	
Circulation: contractor, client organisation, design team	

Figure 9.6   Agenda for site meetings

contract scope of works. The client should not discuss variations directly with the contractor as this is likely to lead to confusion. All communications between the client and contractor and vice versa should be directed via the contract administrator.

As works on site progress and are completed, and in the weeks leading up to the next stage, Stage L – After practical completion – the contract administrator must advise the client to prepare for the change-over in responsibility for insuring and operating the works which will occur at practical completion. This is in addition to liaising with the contractor to ensure that all works will be completed and commissioned to a satisfactory extent to permit practical completion to be achieved.

As noted earlier in the book, practical completion is concerned with the process of handing over the (almost) completed project to the client, be it an entire new building or part of an existing building within an existing and occupied business operation. Practical completion is achieved when the contract administrator issues the Certificate of Practical Completion, signifying that the contractor has achieved, in the view of the contract administrator and the design team, a stage that permits the client to use the project for its intended purpose. In reality, however, there may be a number of minor items that require the contractor's attention, including mechanical systems – air handling plant and so on.

In order that the client organisation may be satisfactorily integrated into the handover process, the contract administrator must organise a formal site handover meeting with appropriate representatives from the contractor, design team and client organisations in attendance. The meeting should include a tour of the works for the client, after which the contractor hands over all keys and the health and safety file to the client. The contract administrator should explain to the client the procedure for

Sources: Combination of *The Architect's Job Book*, 6th edn and RIBA Plan of Work (1973 edition) © RIBA Publications

Figure 9.7   Agenda for handover/practical completion meeting

reporting defects in the works during the defects liability period. Since practical completion handover will involve taking over operational responsibility of all mechanical and electrical plant (air-handling plant, heating and building management and lighting systems and so on), the contractor, client and contract administrator must discuss arrangements well in advance of the handover meeting to ensure appropriate briefing and attendance for client organisation staff. An agenda for the handover/practical completion meeting might be as shown in Figure 9.7 on page 150.

It is important to note that depending on the nature of the project, a number of completion certificates may be required during a project. The above text refers to practical completion of 'the works' rather than parts or stages of the works.

Stage L – After practical completion

Whereas the client's operational involvement with a project is just beginning at this stage, involvement with the project beyond practical completion will, all being well, be minimal for the consultant design team and the contractor. The contractual obligations of the design team should involve overseeing arrangements for negotiating final accounts with the contractor, recording and making good latent defects, and ultimately conclusion of the contract by issue of the final certificate.

Post-project review

Although not included as a specific item within the Plan of Work methodology, a feedback or post-project review process is recommended, and is the subject of the final chapter in this book.

PROGRESS REPORTING FORMATS

In common with earlier stages of the project, during the 'works' project process there is a continuing need for objective reporting methodologies to ensure clear communication throughout the team. Agendas for the pre-contract, pre-start site and regular site meetings have been proposed in this chapter, and the related coordinating client design project management meeting structure was outlined in Chapter 7.

FINANCIAL REPORTING FORMATS

Cost planning and reporting are needed at all stages of the project. From Stage J onwards, however, since it is actual financial commitments which are being reported rather than theoretical cost planning sums, the need for clear reporting is stronger than ever.

The quantity surveyor must be appointed on a basis that permits the provision of monthly cost reports during Phase 3, Construction, Stages J–L. These reports should be circulated to the design team and the client, and will provide invaluable design team information. The reports monitor the financial position relative to the original cost plan established when the contractor was appointed. The tender acceptance sums and estimated final account figures may be usefully included in cost reports where required.

Typically the headings of a cost report will start with the cost plan figures provided by the quantity surveyor and design team at the pre-tender stage, as the client will have made financial provision on this basis. A typical cost report format is shown in Figure 9.8, on page 153.

However, accurate financial data, while essential, do not necessarily communicate clearly the main messages required about finance to the variety of parties who have an interest. To provide meaningful communication these regular cost reports will require further interpretation. For example, there should be a clear and concise bullet point/narrative stating the main areas of change from the previous month's report. This may also involve a separate sheet containing individual reports on the recommended and/or anticipated use of the contingency sum, and a clear record of the financial implications arising from any formally instructed variations to the contract, both additions and deductions.

This further interpretation of the cost reports is not just for client organisations, but for the entire design team. Where clients will be reporting back to their board of management there may also be specific issues to report upon in more detail. For example, reporting requirements for various external sources of funding, various internal budget sources, financial year reporting and so on, should all be clearly specified to the quantity surveyor at an early date, who can then design the reports accordingly.

CHANGE CONTROL MECHANISMS

It is almost inevitable that the requirement to delete works, or for additional works, or for a change to some aspect of the agreed design specified within the contract will present itself during the project. The need for these 'variations' to the contract may arise for many reasons. Perhaps the client organisation board of management introduce a post-tender change to strategic or operational business criteria, or perhaps an unforeseeable event or circumstance arises on site, or a manufacturer makes a specified product obsolete, and so on. The source of the variation may therefore come from any party, yet we have already noted that only the contract administrator can formally instruct the contractor to carry out works that vary in any way from the contract documentation. A process should therefore be established that enables any contributing party to request a variation, have the variation considered on a cost–benefit analysis basis, and for this request to be formally instructed if collectively agreed to be appropriate. The key issue is to ensure that change is controlled in a communicative, project-wide and objectively determined basis. A change control form for project contributors is suggested in Figure 9.9, on page 154.

Ref	Works package	Contractor	Cost plan figure	Accepted tender figure	Variation cost plan/ tender	Estimated final account	Variation: final account/ cost plan	Paid to date	Estimated balance to pay	Notes
1										
2										
3										
4										
5										
6										
7										
8										
9										
10										
Sub-total										
Contingency										
Sub-total										
VAT										
Total										

Figure 9.8   Cost report format

Design change control form

Project title	_____
Date issued	_____
To	Design project manager
From	_____

Job number _____

Date decision required _____

Change proposed

Benefits of change

Reasons for change

Implications of change

For design project manager's use only

Copied to

Implication and effect

Cost	
Programme	
Quality	
Fees	
Other (specify)	

Recommendation

Approve change		Date	
Refuse change		Date	

Figure 9.9   Design change control form

The form should be sent by the originator to the design project manager for circulation, collation of appraisal comments and will be reported on at the design project manager's monthly meetings.

LIAISON AND COORDINATION WITH PARALLEL BUILDINGS CONTRACTS

The previous text applies to any stand-alone design project, whether it is a 'new-build' building, a fit-out contract or a multimedia or graphics project. However, one area which deserves some further thought at this stage relates to projects where two design teams and contract strategies overlap on site in the pursuit of a single overall project objective.

A common situation arises when a multi-trade fit-out contract must begin on site immediately following a multi-trades building shell contract. More likely still is the need for the fit-out contract to begin *before* completion of the shell contract. Managing the site commencement of a fit-out contract in these circumstances is typically as much about managing change as it is about contract management issues. Common issues and questions that arise relate to:

- Responsibility for overall coordination of all activity on site, including health and safety (building snagging, fit-out main contract, client pre-operational activity)
- Responsibility for protecting existing works during subsequent fit-out stages
- Responsibility for ensuring clear distinction of the professional boundaries of design responsibility between the shell infrastructure and the fit-out works
- Responsibility for ensuring clear distinction of professional boundaries of works responsibility between shell infrastructure and fit-out works and the defects liability issues arising.

Typically, there is no 'clean break' completion of the shell contract following which the fit-out works might begin, and hence some form of literal, contractual and management overlap is inevitable. Management issues and strategic choices to be made arise from several generic and typical points as follows:

- The same main contractor carrying out the shell contract works will also tender for the fit-out works
- The fit-out design team will have different lead design consultants and client representatives
- The fit-out works to be carried out have physical implications for aspects of the recently carried-out shell contract infrastructure defects liability responsibilities.

Rather than simplify the overall process by having two parallel teams, with distinctly defined roles providing additional resources, the two-team structure actually requires additional management and communication to ensure coordination of effort. It also requires change management at the point of beginning works on site.

This project interface requires design of an appropriate management process if success is to be achieved. The most successful method of integrating the two project teams is for the client design project manager to communicate priorities to all parties objectively with the full delegated authority of the client's project director/board of management. See Chapter 7 for the design manager meeting agenda and project personnel structure.

A site management procedures manual is an essential and fundamental component. This may typically be structured as shown in Figure 9.10.

Site Management Procedures Manual

Introduction and summary of procedures
Description of overall project, that is, overlap of key personnel and contact information
    Shell contract
    Fit-out contract
    Client organisation
Health and safety on site
Site access
    Parking
    Working hours
Emergency procedures
General arrangement plans
Site welfare
Security
Other project-specific criteria to be included as appropriate

Appendices
    Personnel contact information
    Forms for late/weekend working
    Hot works permits and so on

Figure 9.10   Structure of a site management procedures manual

The procedures manual should be issued to all project contributors by the project director to ensure that it is formally acknowledged as the formal management procedure.

NOTE

1. These reports were: *Constructing the Team* (The Latham Report), Construction Industry Board Working Group Papers, *Constructing Success*, *Briefing the Team*, and *Partnering in the Team*, and *Rethinking Construction* (The Egan Report).

10 Post-project review activity

PURPOSE

The purpose of this chapter is to outline the benefits of conducting a post-project review, and to propose guidelines for carrying it out. While consultants and works contractors involved on the project may carry out their own post-project analysis and keep their own records, the focus here is on reviewing the end result and the project process from the perspective of the client organisation. The objective of the post-project review is to provide improved future business benefits for all parties, through shared objective information for 'continual organisational learning'.

Although not included as a specific item within the RIBA Plan of Work methodology, since 1967,[1] a feedback or post-project review process is recommended for client organisations as a management information resource. Feedback provides an opportunity to review not only the degree of success of the design solution in meeting the brief, but also how successfully the brief was developed, the management issues involved in the process and the performance of the consultant team, the contractors, and the part played by the client representatives in the project process. This will be of most use to clients who have a need for ongoing capital projects. The review process should be open, honest and frank, and perhaps chaired by someone from the client organisation board of management who has not had direct involvement in the project process, to ensure objective analysis. Management and communication procedures should be reviewed. Any difficulties noted with either the project process or the brief, final design, or any mismatch between the brief and the design should be analysed to identify solutions for implementation on future projects. The intention is to communicate 'lessons learned' from the project to enhance the efforts of future project teams, not to find scapegoats to blame for past difficulties.

OUTLINE

- Introduction
- Suggested methodology
- Final account settlement
- Maintenance and latent defects
- Structure of report
- Issue of report.

INTRODUCTION

To simplify the review process and permit the design of a useful and bespoke post-project review, it is essential to start with a simple list of fundamental key areas of concern. The main issue will be an assessment of the success of the finished design measured against the objectives of the brief, but other fundamental issues will relate to management of the various processes, performance of individual contributors and maintenance. The other important issues to consider at the early stages of the post-project review design relate to the timing and the resources that can be made available for carrying out the review.

The stages of a post-project review are shown in Figure 10.1, on page 159.

SUGGESTED METHODOLOGY

Assessing the degree of success of a design project is not as easy as it at first sounds. Many parties have been involved in the project, both within and outside the client organisation, and all will have their own perspective on the degree of success that has been achieved. Many contributors to the project will probably find it difficult to make their assessment of the end result a separate matter from their assessment of the process. The following outline is intended to assist with the design of an appropriate post-project review methodology.

Chairing and leading the post-project review

A member of the client organisation board of management not directly involved in the project should lead the post-project review. When the strategic objectives and the timescale for carrying out the review have been determined, the proposed review methodology should be issued to the project contributors who will be taking part in the review process, for their comment and suggestion. Any pertinent comments or suggestions obtained should be incorporated into the proposed review process and a final 'collective methodology' document issued to the contributors.

When reviewing the success of the project, it is vital that the original brief issued to the design team and the objectives originally identified are referred to. Key questions to be raised relate to satisfaction with the end result: Does the design meet the brief? Was the brief correct?

These issues are closely related and should be treated accordingly. If there is an area of weakness within the design, a review of the brief must be considered in conjunction with a review of the design and the design process. It should be recalled that real success is determined by the degree of business advantage achieved by the project. That this will be reflected in client satisfaction through added sales, visits, or improved costs of manufacture or increased production and so on is clear. However, other success criteria also apply. For example, in addition to increased sales of computers, the design awards

Stage 1   Define strategic objectives and resources

- Appoint a chairperson
- Define the objectives of the post-project review process from the client organisation's perspective
  - The objective may be to some extent generic: 'To review the project design solution and the project process and to distribute conclusions as a means of disseminating "useful lessons" within the organisation for future projects'. The objective may, however, be specific, particularly if there has been a problem. Budget overspend, unsuccessful design solution, programme not achieved and so on
- Define the resources that can be made available
  - Management and staff
  - Finance – for consultant support and so on
  - Time
    The time factor may of course be determined by the objective of the review, particularly if there has been a problem which requires a solution by a given date, for example financial year, disputes which may lead to legal action and so on. It may relate to the setting up of a future project, where staff roles and briefing arrangements are being considered, or where the views of the client organisation's own customers/clients and/or competitors are to be taken into account

Stage 2   Select and prioritise the specific objectives

- Assess the success of the final design relative to the brief.
- Does the design solution satisfy the objectives stated in the brief?
  - Business criteria
    Strategic objectives
    Marketing objectives
    Operational objectives: independent client/customer/visitor surveys? Function, maintenance, revenue costs, energy efficiency and so on
  - Aesthetic criteria
  - Financial criteria
  - Programme criteria
- Was the brief correct? Comprehensive? Consistent? Delivered on time?
- Management issues
  - Briefing
  - Personnel
  - Information/communication
  - Design coordination
  - Works
  - Programme
  - Budget
- Assessing the performance of contributors
  - Staff contributors
    List key personnel
  - Consultants
    List key personnel
  - Works contractors
    List key personnel

Stage 3   Design a simple and realistic post-project review process

- Circulate information
- Hold meetings
- Write and circulate report
- Implement recommendations and conclude process

Each of the above main headings will lead in turn to specific sub-headings depending on the nature of the project/design, the client organisation and so on. The key to a successful review process, as with the main project itself, is to be clear on what is intended in principle at the outset. Viewed like this it is in fact another project, albeit probably of limited duration.

Figure 10.1   Stages of a post-project review

gained by Apple computers for their imac® and PowerBook®/ibook® products and their influence on the design of competitors' products are an important, albeit secondary, indicator of success. In the case of visitor centre/attractions and museum/gallery exhibitions the level of intellectual success of the interpretative design is again a vital, if secondary, indicator of increased visits. Where the design does not meet the business objectives or provide competitive advantage, the reasons for this failure must be explored, starting with an assessment of the brief.

Design review

- List the objectives of the original design brief
- Prioritise these objectives
  - Primary: the business objectives that allow competitive advantage and sustainability of the client organisation
  - Secondary: those that are important, related issues
- Have they been achieved?
- Have the objectives been altered since the client design brief was written? If so, why? When? By whom?
- Have these revised objectives been achieved?

Review of the design brief

- Did the original brief accurately reflect the needs of the organisation?
- Was the brief clear in terms of business objectives and priorities?
- Was the brief consistent?
- Was briefing information supplied on time?
- Were any changes to *key objectives* in the brief required during the process?
- Why were changes required?
- Could the brief have been improved?
- What changes, if any, should be made to future design briefs and design brief development processes?

Management of the project

The many aspects of management required during the project should be reviewed. Where a design project has achieved its objectives without any major difficulties the review may indicate key areas of management strengths which have made the success achievable. It may also identify areas of potential risk through aspects of management which were weak on the project. Both will provide valuable insights for future teams.

Where a design project has encountered problems or has ended in some difficulty the review should identify the areas of weakness to be assessed on future projects. The process for appointing the consultant team should be reviewed, from shortlisting through to the success of the contractual arrangements. The issues noted should remain impersonal and not identify personnel as far as possible. The review could perhaps be concluded with a 'SWOT analysis' type format (as set out in Chapter 4).

Management Review

Following discussion with project colleagues and client organisation board of management, the project director should write a brief narrative summarising the key aspects of management on this project.

It is suggested that the following headings are used as prompts and given marks out of 10.

	Score	Comments
Success of Design		
Briefing		
Process for appointing consultants		
Personnel		
Consultants		
Staff		
Contractors		
Information/communication		
Design coordination		
Contracts		
Works		
Programme		
Budget		
Total		

SWOT analysis	Strengths	Weaknesses
	Opportunities	Threats

This report prepared by _____ Project manager/project director

Figure 10.2   Form for collating management information

A form for collating management information is suggested as in Figure 10.2, on page 161; this summarises and integrates the separate performance reviews of consultants, contractors and client organisation staff.

Performance review: consultants

Some key issues may be raised here. However, it is suggested that the most useful method is to keep a brief standardised form which may be included as an appendix in the post-project review, and may also be kept separately as a database within the client organisation for distribution/availability to inform any future shortlisting process (see Figure 10.3, on page 163). The performance review data may be integrated into the overall management review. Note that different headings may be used for differing consultants; for example a review of lead consultant's overall design leadership and coordination of technical information will not be required for sub-consultants, and so on.

Performance review: contractors and suppliers

A review of the performance of the works contractor may be carried out in a similar fashion (see Figure 10.4, on page 164).

Performance review: client staff

It will also be worthwhile to keep a brief record of how members of staff from the client organisation have performed during the project. This may be achieved either through the use of a brief standardised form as in Figures 10.3 and 10.4, or by using the annual staff review process undertaken by the client organisation. The views of both the members of staff involved and their line managers should be taken into account. Where staff members have core business roles other than working on capital projects, and have been only partially involved in a project, it will be of value to seek their views on the degree of difficulty in carrying out both roles simultaneously. Additionally, particularly where a client organisation will be undertaking further design projects, staff views should be gathered on the following:

- Organisational issues
  - Timescale adequate? Problematic?
  - Budget adequate? Problematic?
  - Support given by employer/line manager during the project adequate? Room for improvement?
  - Conflict between core business role and project role?
  - Training needs for further projects?
  - Views on other staff involved – Communication skills and so on
- Project issues
  - Views on the briefing process

Name	Consultant's practice name
Address	Consultant's address
Phone	Consultant's phone number
Contact	Name of consultant's partner/director/associate
Project	Name of project
Fee	£******.**
Works value	£******.**
Fee as % of works	**.*%

Performance Report

Overall performance — Following discussion with project colleagues and client organisation board of management, the project director should write a brief narrative summarising the key aspects of the consultant's performance on this project.

It is suggested that the following headings are used as prompts and given marks out of 10.

	Score	Comments
Creative skills		
Design leadership		
Technical skills		
Detailing		
Information coordination		
Management skills		
Project management		
Budget management		
Contract management		
Reliability		
Other		
Overall performance		
Total		

This report prepared by _____   Project manager/project director

Figure 10.3   Form for consultant's performance review

Name	Contractor's business name
Address	Contractor's address
Phone	Contractor's phone number
Contact	Name of contractor's partner/director/associate Name of site personnel
Project	Name of project
Tender award value	£******.**
Final account value	£******.**
Sum as % of works	*.**%

Performance Report

Overall performance — *Following discussion with project colleagues and client organisation board of management, the project director should write a brief narrative summarising the key aspects of the consultant's performance on this project.*

It is suggested that the following headings are used as prompts and given marks out of 10.

	Score	Comments
Management skills		
Reliability		
Site management		
Workmanship		
Programme		
Other		
Overall performance		
Total		

This report prepared by _____   Project manager/project director

Figure 10.4   Form for contractor's performance review

- Views on the project development and management process
- Views on the finished design
- Views on the consultants
- Views on the contractors.

FINAL ACCOUNT SETTLEMENT

At the end of a design project it is most unlikely that each of the works packages will have progressed from tender acceptance stage without any variation or change. The reasons for changes will vary from 'internally controlled' design intent, either a client or consultant request for change, to 'externally controlled' pragmatic instructions necessary to deal with unforeseen circumstances arising on site or from another external source. Faced with change of any description, it will be difficult to reach an objectively reasoned final account settlement without clear contract administration records.

For works contracts, the key controls will be the regular financial reports produced by the quantity surveyor, the list of contract administrator's instructions and other change control documentation. As noted in Chapter 8, the financial reports should track the financial implications of variations step by step, also stating briefly the reasons for the required variation, and will assist in providing a platform for reasoned analysis and negotiation. Each variation to a contract requires a formal 'instruction' to be issued by the contract administrator.

Where client organisations have a query over one or other of the variations/ instructions, specific reports should be requested from the contract administrator/lead design consultant. It is likely, though, that adequate information will already exist as part of the change control process, assuming this has been adequately designed and properly implemented as noted earlier in this book.

Problems and claims – how to resolve them

Upon practical completion of a project, a final account will ideally be submitted promptly by the main contractor to the quantity surveyor and contract administrator. This should be a figure that can be agreed by the design team and client organisation without difficulty. Typically some degree of negotiation may be required over some items, but generally the project has remained within the financial parameters expected by all parties. However, what happens where this is not the case? While all works contracts claim situations are unique, the following general principles may assist in successful negotiation.

The often-used 'claim' term is not a formally defined or recognised contract term. A claim will usually arise where a contractor asserts or claims additional payment for 'direct loss and/or expense' under the terms of the contract. Claims under this heading fall into two categories – extensions of time (prolongation claim) and loss or expense for disruption to the regular progress of the works (disruption claim). Both are for what they say, that is, payment for direct loss and associated expenses and no more! It is not an opportunity to make additional profit.

Where there is a disagreement regarding the financial outcome of a contract, resulting in a claim being made by the contractor, there are several factors which will influence the approach to be taken to resolve the situation. First, some points of principle to consider are:

- Clear and concise information is vital to achieving an objective analysis of any situation. Conclusions and recommendations based on analysis of fact are required, not opinions.
- Assuming that comprehensive tender information has been prepared, if no changes are made to the design after tenders are awarded, the cost agreed at the tender award stage shouldn't change either. Good change control management is therefore essential in controlling variations as they arise, and, where required, to rule variations out before they become contractual instructions. Where a variation *is* agreed and instructed, good change control management is essential in maintaining the clear information required for subsequent objective assessment and negotiation.
- Resolving a disagreement without recourse to legal advice is recommended wherever possible. In addition to payment of legal and professional fees, client organisations must also consider the opportunity cost/loss of productive staff time required to pursue/defend claims. Legal disputes require considerable time and financial resources. In fact, where there is a dispute it is often the 'cooling factor' of time that leads to negotiation of a final outcome. As time passes, personnel on all sides often move on, leading to a change in attitude on the part of one or all organisations.

The four key factors influencing the approach to be taken are:

1 *The size of the claim.* The size of a claim for additional payment is of course the main issue when negotiating a final account claim, as it will undoubtedly affect the other issues noted. The approach taken in resolving a dispute over hundreds of pounds will be quite different from that required to resolve a dispute over tens of thousands, or even millions of pounds.
2 *The attitude of the contractor.* To a large extent, a contractor's attitude to making claims, will be known at the outset and should be one of the factors taken into account when appointing a successful contractor, all discussed in earlier chapters. Where it is known from the outset that a design project has the potential for variation, say where a client and design team are seeking a unique one-off design with innovative aspects functionally, visually or with materials and detailing/ construction technique, selecting a contractor who is known to treat variations objectively, rather than in an exploitative manner, is a key factor.
3 *The attitude of the design team members.* The attitude of the design team members to a claim may vary for a number of reasons. First, they may often feel potentially in the front line of blame for any variation and may therefore take a stance that is defensive rather than truly objective. The reality is that a defensive counter-attack to that taken

by the contractor will not assist in moving towards a conclusion. Where a position on a claim differs radically from a contractor's version of events, this must be clearly and objectively set out.

4 *The attitude of the client organisation.* To arrive at an effective position relative to any final account claim, the attitude adopted by the client organisation must arise from an objective synthesis of all of the above factors. Beyond that, where disagreement remains, a process of negotiation is required. To arrive at an objective initial position, start by requesting the relevant financial data from the quantity surveyor. This will state the two figures put forward by the contractor and by the design team. The design team figure will be an assessment prepared by the quantity surveyor based on the rates provided by the contractor's tender and other relevant information supplied by the other design team members. Finally, it should be remembered that any claim is for 'direct loss and or expenses' only, and accordingly full substantiation is required from any contractor within their financial data. An offer may be made based on analysis of the facts which seek an acceptable 'middle ground' (see Figure 10.5).

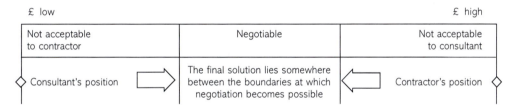

Figure 10.5   Negotiating an acceptable offer

MAINTENANCE AND LATENT DEFECTS

There are two aspects relating to maintenance which are worthy of some further consideration:

1 The relationship between design and maintenance.
2 The difference between maintenance and making good of latent defects.

There is an obvious relationship between design and maintenance. In many ways it is the same inevitable relationship as that between the brief and the design. Providing staff and other resources for adequate maintenance of a new facility must be considered by client organisations before completion and operation of the project. Indeed, maintenance issues should be evaluated and discussed as part of the operational briefing and design development stages, and should inform design decisions. There is no point in having a design prepared that cannot be adequately maintained. Obvious issues are security, building fabric and mechanical and electrical plant maintenance, cleaning and replacement of lamps or other 'consumables', plus staffing and appropriate revenue finances. While basic maintenance should not lead the decision-making process, it should be part of the mix and must inform both the operational planning and the client design brief. Figure 10.6 illustrates.

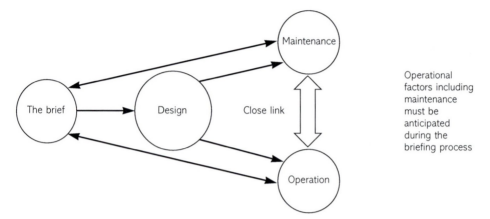

Figure 10.6   Maintenance as part of the overall mix

Since the introduction of the Construction Design and Management regulations, known as the 'CDM regulations', aspects of maintenance have become more explicitly a part of the earlier design development process. Although the design team now have a legal responsibility to consider the construction, operation and maintenance inherent in a design solution, they will simply specify what is required, not consider the resourcing implications on an operational basis.

It is also important to distinguish between maintenance issues and latent defects. From the date at which practical completion is achieved, the client organisation must maintain the new project items on an operational basis. The term 'latent defects' relates to items that have not been carried out in accordance with the contract documents and that might not have been possible to detect or foresee at an earlier stage. It does not require the contractor to return to site to rectify damage that is caused by staff or the public using the design.

STRUCTURE OF REPORT

The format of the post-project review report should follow standard report-writing methodology. It should be as concise as possible, keeping support detail for the appendices. The report must be read, but, more important, it must be understood. The structure should be as follows:

- Preliminary text
  - Executive summary or abstract (1–2 pages)
  - Summary of main conclusions and recommendations (1 page)
  - Contents/tables/illustrations (1 page)
- Main text (page quantity as required)

  – Introduction
  – Analysis of information
  – Detailed conclusions
  – Detailed recommendations
* References and appendices (page quantity as required)
  – Project directory
  – Contributors to the review
  – Supporting reports and data (key project records and so on)
  – Bibliography if required.

These headings may be expanded as follows.

Preliminary text

To a very large degree the preliminary section of the report should tell the reader everything they need to know about the scope of the report and should be able to stand alone. To achieve this it must be clear and concise. To this end it is suggested that no more than two pages are used to summarise the reasons for the report, its intended outcomes, its methodology, and its main conclusions and recommendations.

Main text

Introduction

The introduction must tell the reader all that they need to know to understand the rest of the report. There should be a broad statement regarding the background to the report, and perhaps the design project itself, and the objectives to be addressed during the review. The assessment methodology should be outlined and the structure of the report given. Any limitations inherent in the report – for example issues of commercial confidentiality – should be stated.

Analysis of information

This section presents the findings of the assessment. They should be objectively and concisely stated and structured in a logical and sequential manner appropriate to the needs of the review. The structure will vary depending on the nature of the client organisation and the nature and scale of the project.

Detailed conclusions

The conclusions and recommendations are the key aspects of any report. Collectively they provide objective instructions for taking structured action. The conclusions relative to each section of the review, and the objectives outlined in the introduction, should be given in order of importance. Conclusions state what the results of the analysis mean. Conclusions, not opinions, are essential.

Contributor	Contact	Address	Phone	E-mail	Web
Client organisation team					
Project director					
Design project manager					
Estates					
Head of finance					
Operations					
Consultant team					
Lead design consultant					
Structural engineer					
M&E engineer					
Quantity surveyor					
Graphic design					
Multimedia design					
Audiovisual design					
Works contractors					
Main contractor					
Project director					
Project manager					
Surveyor					
Site manager					
Subcontractors					
Works package 1					
Works package 2					
Works package 3					
Contractors employed by client					
Direct contractor 1					
Direct contractor 2					
Direct contractor 3					
Suppliers					
Supplier 1					
Supplier 2					
Supplier 3					

Figure 10.7   Form for project directory information

Detailed recommendations

The recommendations for action relative to the conclusions should be stated in order of priority and a precise timescale for achieving each recommendation should be given. Recommendations state 'actions required' based on the results of the analysis.

References and appendices

The references and appendices section should contain all supporting information obtained during the review process, including relevant design drawings, management and performance reviews, final cost reports and analysis and so on. Any questionnaires or consultant reports and any relevant technical data should be included, as should a personnel directory. Each type of reference material should be contained in a separate appendix.

The project directory information may be structured as shown in Figure 10.7, on page 170.

ISSUE OF REPORT

The post-project review report and project directory should be issued to client organisation board of management, seeking their support of and implementation of the recommendations. Project contributors should receive copies of the report before the formal issue to permit their acknowledgement and support of the final recommendations. Where there is dissent, this should be noted when the final report is submitted.

NOTE

1. S. Cox, et al., *The Architect's Job Book*, 6th edn, London: RIBA Publications, 1995.

Bibliography

Chappell, D. and Willis, A. (2000), *The Architect in Practice, Eighth Edition*, London: Blackwell Science Ltd.

Compiled Phillips, R. (2000), *The Architect's Plan of Work*, ed. S. Lupton and F. Ringrose, London: RIBA Publications.

Construction Industry Board (2000), *Selecting Consultants for the Team: Balancing Quality and Price, Second Edition*, London: Thomas Telford Publishing.

Cox, S. and others (1995), *Architect's Job Book, Sixth Edition*, ed. S. Cox, A. Hamilton, London: RIBA Publications.

The Creative Industries Taskforce (1998), *Creative Industries Mapping Document*, London: Department for Culture, Media and Sport.

Design Council (2000), *Design in Britain 2000/2001*, London: Design Council.

Dry, D. (1983), *The Interior Design Handbook*, London: Architecture and Building Practice Guides Ltd.

Egan, Sir J. (1998), *Rethinking Construction*, London Department of the Environment, Transport and the Regions.

Freeman, C. (1983), *Design and British Economic Performance*, Lecture given at the Design Centre, London, 23 March.

Latham, Sir Michael (1994), *Constructing the Team*, HMSO.

McMillan and MacFarlane (1991), *Scottish Business Law*, London: Pitman Publishing.

Sentence, A. and Clarke, J. (1997), *The contribution of design to the UK economy*, London: Design Council.

Thomson, G. and others (1993), *Managing the UK*, ed. R. Maidment and G. Thomson, London: Sage Publications.

Tuckman, B. W. (1965), 'Developmental sequences in small groups', *Psychological Bulletin*, 63, 384–99.

OTHER USEFUL BOOKS

Billington, M. (2001), *Manual to the Building Regulations*, London: HMSO Books.

Blyth, A. and Worthington, J. (2001), *Managing the Brief for Better Design*, London: Spon Press.

Byrom, R. (2002), *Construction Companion: Briefing*, London: RIBA Publications.

Carmichael, S. (2002), *A Guide to Successful Client Relationships*, London: RIBA Enterprises.

— (2000), *Working with consultants*, London: RIBA Publications.

— (2000), *Painless Financial Management and Job Costing*, London: RIBA Publications.

— (1999), *The Architect's contract. A guide to RIBA Forms of Appointment 1999 and other Architect's appointments*, London: RIBA Publications.

— (1996), Design Management Systems BS7000 Part 4, London: British Standards Institution.

Chapman, R. (2002), *Retaining Design Team Members: A risk management approach*, London: RIBA Enterprises.

Chappell, D., Greenstreet, R. and Dunn, M. (2002), *Legal and Contractual Procedures for Architects*, London: Architectural Press.

Cornes, D. and Winward, R. (2002), *Winward Fearon on Collateral Warranties*, London: Blackwell Science.

Hyams, D. (2001), *Construction Companion: Briefing*, London: RIBA Publications.

Morton, R. (2002), *Construction UK: Introduction to the Industry*, London: Blackwell Science.

Robertson, S. (2001), *Construction Companion: Feasibility Studies*, London: RIBA Publications.

CASE STUDY CONTRIBUTORS

Contact	Practice	Discipline
Neil Wilson	MKW Design Partnership	Exhibition Design
Lizzie Sanders	McKinstrie Wilde Millhouse	Graphic Design
Graham Russell	The Northcross Group	Multidisciplinary
Stephen Richards	The National Museums of Scotland	Development Manager
Derek Hodgson	Derek Hodgson Associates	Product Design
Kevan Shaw	Kevan Shaw Lighting Design	Lighting
Mike Spearman	The Multimedia Team	Multimedia
David MacRitchie	Page and Park	Architecture

Further information

- Chartered Society of Designers
  5 Bermondsey Exchange
  179–181 Bermondsey Street
  London SE1 3UW
  Tel 020 7357 8088
  www.csd.org.uk

- Royal Institute of British Architects
  66 Portland Place
  London
  W1N 4AD
  Tel 020 7580 5533
  www.architecture.com

- Royal Institution of Chartered Surveyors
  12 Great George Street
  Parliament Square
  London
  SW1P 3AD
  Tel 020 7222 7000
  www.rics.org.uk

- Royal Town Planning Institute
  41 Botolph Lane
  London
  EC3R 8DL
  Tel 020 7929 9494
  www.rtpi.org.uk

- Institution of Structural Engineers
  11 Upper Belgrave Street
  London
  SW1X 8BH
  Tel 020 7235 4535
  www.istructe.org.uk

- Institution of Civil Engineers
  1–7 Great George Street
  London
  SW1P 3AA
  Tel 020 7222 7722
  www.ice.org.uk

- Institution of Lighting Engineers
  Lennox House
  9 Lawford Road
  Rugby
  Warwickshire
  CV21 2DZ
  Tel 01788 576492
  www.ile.org.uk

- Institution of Mechanical Engineers
  1 Birdcage Walk
  London
  SW1H 9JJ
  www.imeche.org.uk

- Institution of Electrical Engineers
  Savoy Place
  London
  WC2R 0BL
  Tel 020 7240 1871
  www.iee.org.uk

- The Landscape Institute
  6–7 Barnard Mews
  London
  SW11 1QU
  Tel 020 7350 5200
  www.l-i.org.uk

- British Property Federation
  1 Warwick Row
  7th Floor
  London
  SW1E 5ER
  Tel 020 7828 0111
  www.bpf.org.uk

- Design Business Association
  35–39 Old Street
  London
  EC1V 9HX
  Tel 020 7251 9229
  www.dba.org.uk

- Design Council
  34 Bow Street
  London
  WC2E 7DL
  Tel 020 7420 5200
  www.designcouncil.org.uk

- Association for Project Management
  Thornton House
  150 West Wycombe Road
  High Wycombe
  HP12 3AE
  Tel 01494 440090
  www.apm.org.uk

- Stationery Office
  PO Box 29
  Norwich
  NR3 1GN
  Tel 0870 600 5522
  www.clicktso.com

- The Institute of Planning Supervisors
  Heriot-Watt Research Park
  Edinburgh
  EH14 4AP
  Tel 0131 449 4646
  www.planningsupervisors.org.uk

- Design Management Institute
  29 Temple Place (Second Floor)
  Boston
  MA 02111-1350 USA
  Tel 617 338 6380
  www.dmi.org

Index